Remaking Birmingham

Remaking Birmingham focuses on the visual culture of urban regeneration as a key context for understanding the remaking of the city. It brings together practising architects, artists, photographers and academics who represent and comment on the city as a visual environment in which perception contributes profoundly to regeneration.

The contributors explore the relationships between historical and contemporary ways of seeing and representing change in Birmingham. They consider how the design and building of the cityscape encode visual understandings of urban space; how the relationship between the built environment and social process is mediated by the visual forms of the city; how strategies for rebranding the city impact upon its broader visual economy; and how planners, architects, artists and image-makers participate in urban representation and redevelopment. They also address the need to visualize new ideas of place and community within post-industrial urbanism.

The volume is multidisciplinary in content, including contributions from specialists in architecture, public and community arts, photography, and urban studies – their critical perspectives linked by interest in urban visual culture. The book aims to contribute to practical and critical understandings of the relations between design, regeneration and the arts in contemporary urbanism. The city of Birmingham and its environs provide a rich case study for such concerns as this once major industrial city strives to build a new city image amidst an uncertain post-industrial future.

The book reflects upon and extends current debates about urban regeneration, the design of public space, and the role of arts in urban redevelopment.

Liam Kennedy is Head of Department of American and Canadian Studies, University of Birmingham. He teaches undergraduate and postgraduate courses on American Urbanism, comparative urbanism, representations of the city in film and photography. His research and publications have been in the fields of urban studies and visual culture, including monographs (*Susan Sontag, Race and Urban Space in American Culture*); edited books (*Urban Space and Representation, City Sites: Multimedia Essays on New York and Chicago* [2000]), plus many articles on urban culture and representation.

Other titles available from Spon and Routledge

The Enterprising City Centre
Manchester's Development Challenge
Gwyn Williams

Towards an Urban Renaissance
The Urban Task Force

Urban Future 21
A Global Agenda for Twenty-First Century Cities
Peter Hall and Ulrich Pfeiffer

The Chosen City
Nicholas Schoon

Cities for the New Millennium
Edited by Marcial Echenique and Andrew Saint

Forthcoming:

Transforming Barcelona
Edited by Tim Marshall

For further information and to order from our online catalogue
visit our website at www.sponpress.com

Remaking Birmingham

The visual culture of urban regeneration

Edited by Liam Kennedy

Routledge
Taylor & Francis Group

LONDON AND NEW YORK

First published 2004 by Routledge
2 Park Square, Milton Park, Abingdon, Oxon OX14 4RN

Simultaneously published in the USA and Canada
by Routledge
270 Madison Avenue, New York, NY 10016

Routledge is an imprint of the Taylor & Francis Group

© 2004 Liam Kennedy, selection and editorial; individual chapters, the
contributors

Typeset in Univers by Florence Production, Stoodleigh, Devon
Printed and bound in Great Britain by TJ International, Padstow, Cornnwall

British Library Cataloguing in Publication Data
A catalogue record for this book is available from the British Library

Library of Congress Cataloging in Publication Data
Remaking Birmingham: the visual culture of urban regeneration/edited
by Liam Kennedy.
        p. cm.
    Includes bibliographical references and index.
    ISBN 0–415–28838–X (hardcover : alk. paper) – ISBN 0–415–28839–8
    (pbk. : alk. paper)
1. City planning–England–Birmingham. 2. Urban renewal–England–
Birmingham. 3. Birmingham (England) I. Kennedy, Liam, 1946–
NA9187.B57R45 2004
711′.4′0942496–dc22   2003023944

ISBN   0–415–28838–X (hb)
        0–415–28839–8 (pb)

Contents

Acknowledgements

This volume emerges from speculative discussions with architects, artists, and others who have been involved in the visual regeneration of Birmingham in recent years. Several of these discussions gave momentum and shape to the making of the volume – particular thanks to Joe Holyoak, Pete James, and Sylvia King. I am grateful to Arts Council England, West Midlands (Caroline Foxhall) and Birmingham City Council (Sylvia Broadley) for funding support. Thanks, too, to Steve Rea at University of Birmingham for aid with the illustrations. Maria Balshaw has profoundly influenced my relation to and understanding of Birmingham, including the making of this volume – I am grateful for this and for the creative ways in which she remakes this city as home.

Notes on Contributors

Will Alsop founded Alsop Architects in 1979 and has executed such major commissions as the Hôtel du Département des Bouches du Rhône, Marseilles (1994), Cardiff Bay Barrage (1997), North Greenwich Underground Station (1999), Peckham Library (2000) – Winner of the RIBA Stirling Prize – and is currently working on projects in the UK, Spain, Canada, Singapore and the Netherlands, where a second office was established in 2001.

Maria Balshaw is the Director of Creative Partnerships Birmingham – seconded from the University of Birmingham where she worked in the Department of American and Canadian Studies. She is the author of *Looking for Harlem* (2000), the co-editor of *Urban Space and Representation* (1999) and editor and co-author of *City Sites: Multimedia Essays on New York and Chicago* (2000) at www.citysites.org.uk

Vanley Burke has lived in Birmingham since 1965 and has been photographing the African-Caribbean community around him since then. In recent years he has documented Asian and other communities who have settled in the city and the growing archive of his work – held by Birmingham Central Library – is an important record of the city's cultural history. His work has been published widely and shown in major exhibitions across the world.

Justin Edgar is a writer, director and producer who was born and brought up in Birmingham. He directed the feature film *Large* (2001), which remains the only feature shot and set entirely in the city. He is currently making a short film entitled *Round*, set in the Rotunda building in central Birmingham.

Graham Gussin has been exhibiting internationally since the early 1990s. Recent solo exhibitions include: Venice Biennale (2003), Ikon Gallery, Birmingham (2002), New Museum of Contemporary Art, New York (2001), Tate Gallery, London (1998). In 2001 Gussin was curator of *Nothing* with Ele Carpenter, presented at the Northern Gallery for Contemporary Arts, Sunderland, CAC Vilnius and Rooseum, Malmö.

Tim Hall is Senior Lecturer in Geography at the University of Gloucestershire. He is the author of *Urban Geography* (2001) and co-editor of *The Entrepreneurial City* (1998), *The City Cultures Reader* (2000) and *Urban Futures* (2003).

Joe Holyoak is an architect and urban designer, and Reader at Birmingham School of Architecture and Landscape, University of Central England. From 1988 to 1995 he campaigned with the pressure group Birmingham for People for public space in the redevelopment of the Bull Ring.

Glenn Howells is the founding director of Glenn Howells Architects, which has offices in Birmingham and London. The practice was established in 1990 and has won several national and international competitions and awards. Academic experience includes visiting tutor at Nottingham, Plymouth, Belfast and Bath University. In addition, Glenn Howells is chair of the West Midlands Architecture Centre, Midlands Architecture and the Designed Environment (MADE) and a regional advisor for the Commission for Architecture and the Built Environment (CABE).

Peter James is Head of Photographs at Birmingham Central Library where he is responsible for one of the national collections of photography. He has curated exhibitions of historical and contemporary photography and has published books and articles relating to the history of photography in Birmingham, including *Coming to Light* (1998).

Liam Kennedy is Senior Lecturer and Head of Department of American and Canadian Studies at the University of Birmingham. His research interests include American and British urbanism and visual studies. He is the author of *Race and Urban Space in American Culture* (2000), co-editor of *Urban Space and Representation* (2000) and of *City Sites: Multimedia Essays on New York and Chicago* (2000).

Deborah Kermode joined the Ikon Gallery as a curator in 1996 and was responsible for developing the education programme together with Ikon's small-scale touring exhibitions. In 1999 she became Ikon's first curator of off-site projects.

Sylvia King is Chief Executive of The Public, based in West Bromwich in the West Midlands, and an acknowledged international authority on community arts practice. The Public Building is the organization's £40 million flagship project, designed by internationally acclaimed Alsop Architects, at the heart of the £250 million regeneration of Sandwell.

Jane Lutz is based at the Centre for Urban and Regional Studies in the University of Birmingham. Her main interests are in city cultures, culture and regeneration, the creative industries, and place-marketing. She was part of the small team that put together the bid for Birmingham to become European Capital of Culture in 2008.

Deborah Parsons lectures in twentieth-century English literature at the University of Birmingham. Her research interests focus on the cultures and representations of urban modernity. She is the author of *Streetwalking the Metropolis* (2000) and *A Cultural History of Madrid* (2003).

Dave Pollard is a builder who has worked internationally and has returned to Birmingham to find ways to express himself through 'interventions' in the built environment at a time of massive transformation in the city. He is a member of the Sozo Collective.

Nigel Prince is an independent curator and writer. Curatorial projects include: *In the Midst of Things* (with Gavin Wade), Bournville (1999); Andrea Zittel, *A-Z Cellular Compartment Units*, The Mailbox/Ikon Gallery, Birmingham, Andrea Rosen Gallery, New York (2001–2); *Recompositions: Reverse Music*, Graham Gussin with Mark Lockett, Ikon Gallery and Birmingham Conservatoire (2002).

Wendy Shillam is a partner in Shillam + Smith Architecture and Urbanism. The practice has been working in Birmingham for several years.

Illustration credits

Alsop Architects 5.1, 5.3, colour plates 5, 6

Birmingham Central Library, Introduction picture 2, 2.2, 11.1, 11.2, 11.3, 11.4, 11.6, colour plates 1, 9, 10, 11, 12

Birmingham City Council Planning Department 1.7, 1.8, 1.9, 1.10

Birmingham for People 1.3, 1.4, 1.5, 1.6

Julian Bull 10.1, 10.2

Vanley Burke 14.1, 14.2, 14.3, 14.4, 14.5, 14.6, 14.7, 14.8, 14.9, 14.10, 14.11, 14.12, 14.13, 14.14, 14.15, 14.16, 14.17, 14.18

Justin Edgar 12.1

Ikon Gallery 8.1

Halcyon Gallery colour plates 2, 3, 15

Graham Gussin and Nigel Prince 9.1–9.80

Tim Hall 7.1, colour plate 7

Glenn Howells Architects 4.1, 4.2

Jubilee Arts 6.1, 6.2, 6.3, 6.4

Liam Kennedy Introduction picture 6

Gary Kirkham 8.2, 8.3

H. A. Mason/Birmingham Central Library 1.1

Tom Merilion 15.2

Midland Area Housing 10.4

Ming de Nasty colour plate 13

Dave Pollard 10.3

Public Works Department/Birmingham Central Library 1.2

Shillam + Smith 3.1, 3.3, colour plate 4

David Gasca Tucker I.4, 2.1, 2.3, 2.4, 2.5, 5.2

Stan's Cafe 15.3

Stan's Cafe/Creative Partnerships 15.4

Luke Unsworth 11.5

Chris Webb colour plate 8

Introduction

The Creative Destruction of Birmingham

Liam Kennedy

Interviewed in this volume about his links with Birmingham and the region, the architect Will Alsop remarks:

> I remember Birmingham being the epitome of modernity. I remember people making movies about the wonders of the car being this moving platform from which to view the city. Birmingham was the future – in a sense it has been the future, but that bit of the future is worn out now and we need a new one.

The Birmingham that Alsop remembers is the city that embraced utopian visions of modernist urban planning in the middle of the twentieth century: it bulldozed historic urban fabrics and built high-rise towers; it dedicated itself to the motor car and pressed pedestrians into subways; it championed mechanization, mass production and the rational engineering of urban community. In the post-war period, Birmingham undertook comprehensive redevelopment projects with a zeal unwitnessed in any other British city. Writing in 1970, Anthony Sutcliffe observed that 'Much of the city's attraction lay in its almost transatlantic modernity . . . In Birmingham action had replaced talk . . . and laid the foundations of one of the most visually dynamic and exciting cities in Britain, if not in Europe' (Sutcliffe 1970: 473). Since the 1970s, of course, Birmingham has been closely identified with the failures of the modernist project. As this urbanism became discredited, so Birmingham became the British symbol of its social and aesthetic failures, a dystopian lesson in urban decline – reviled for its concrete brutalism and its disdain for the pedestrian, it became a focus for anti-urban sentiment.[1] Whether figured as utopian or dystopian, Birmingham's transatlantic modernity is characterized by its commitment to waves of creative destruction: compulsively levelling and rebuilding the urban landscape in the image of an imagined urban future. The post-war modernism was a first attempt at creating a

I.1
**Family group by tower blocks,
Perry Barr, Birmingham, 1967**
Photo Nick Hedges

twenty-first-century city. Today, a fresh attempt is well under way, building on – but also seeking to bury – the 'concrete dreams'[2] of the first.

Birmingham is a city with a long, uneven history of ambitious industrial and urban planning. Its transatlantic modernity precedes the mid-twentieth century, having roots in its nineteenth-century commitments to innovation in manufacturing and progressive municipal governance. The drive to erase and rebuild was already evident in Joseph Chamberlain's Improvement Scheme of the 1870s and has continued to characterize the city's development since its incorpration in 1889 (when it adopted the motto 'Forward') and feed the utopian rhetorics of city leaders. Birmingham's creative destruction is a compelling urban drama in which the dialectics of erasure and renewal are forever being played out. The Inner Ring Road, a masterpiece of design and planning in many respects, was intended to liberate, to create movement in and through the city – instead, it became the 'concrete collar' that had to be broken if the city was to breathe again. Of course, this is a universal point – planning is transformative but also repressive – but in Birmingham it has deeper resonance than in most British cities and is indicative of the city's transatlantic associations. Unlike most British and European cities, Birmingham does not have a defined historical centre – its core has been hollowed out in the American fashion and it has long lacked morphological definition in landscape design and iconographic definition in its architecture. This lack of definition is a key reason for the common perception of Birmingham as 'a non-place bounded by motorways' (Chatwin 1997: 12), and for its ongoing efforts to come to terms with its creative destruction. As Stuart Jeffries wryly observes: 'You should go to Birmingham to see the drama of a city, all-too-visibly, in an eternal struggle with itself' (Jeffries 2000: 17).

Birmingham's current wave of remaking is not principally defined as a project of urban planning and building. Rather, in line with so many other urban centres, it is looking to culture and consumption to drive regeneration and advertise an image that will attract investment and tourism.[3] Cities that aspire to compete in global markets tend to accentuate their symbolic economies: making use of culture and the arts to promote the city image, supporting 'flagship' architectural projects and designing spectacular shopping and entertainment attractions. In the mid-1980s regeneration plans began to be laid along these lines in Birmingham and they took on fresh impetus and focus following the seminal Highbury Initiative in 1988, when an international gathering of planners, architects and urbanists met to discuss a 'vision for the city' – a key finding was that 'the city has no clear

I.2
Retaining wall, The Bull Ring, 2001
Photo Mike Hallett

I.3
Brindleyplace, Birmingham, 2003

visual image' (Chatwin 1997: 12). A comprehensive master plan for central city regeneration was drawn up and has been followed through with some resolve despite occasional political wranglings. A key lever has been the introduction of entrepreneurial modes of governance in the city, encouraging private and public sectors to work in partnership on regeneration projects. The £1.5 billion redevelopment of the city centre has been supported by massive investment in flagship projects (such as Brindleyplace), the renovation of iconic industrial buildings (such as the Custard Factory, the Mailbox and Fort Dunlop), and a major investment in public arts programmes. The city centre is being rebuilt in terms of 'Quarters', each to be connected by walkways and a necklace of public squares – a revaluing of pedestrianization as called for by the Highbury report and a symbolic effort to undo the image of 'motor city'.

Birmingham's current redevelopment mimics key features of the so-called 'new urbanism' of postmodern planning and design and is indicative of a drive to manufacture a sense of urbanity. Entrepreneurial efforts to establish a coherent and promotable image for the city have emphasized urbanity as an essential product of regeneration and signifier of renewed urban vitality; for local politicians, it has the added edge of suggesting an expansion of urban citizenship. These are all good things but they are not necessarily the result of 'urban regeneration', whatever the ideals of its

I.4
Future Systems' Selfridges building, Birmingham, under construction, 2003

proponents. As many commentators have pointed out, the ideal of urbanity has most coherent and directed appeal to sectors of the middle classes (as a promise to re-enchant their image of the city as a space of community) even though it appears to naturalize the desires of a broader urban citizenry (see Robins 1994). The question of *whose* image is being projected and served by urban regeneration in Birmingham is an important but muted concern, overshadowed by the rhetoric and impetus of regeneration. This is not a question of identifying the (in)authentic Birmingham, rather, it is an issue of understanding the relationships between urban forms and social values, as these shape issues of access, belonging and citizenship within the public culture of the city.

It is also an issue of visuality, of conditions and ways of seeing (see Balshaw and Kennedy 2000). The commercial imagineering of the new Birmingham involves an intensification of aesthetic concerns in consideration of urban forms. This is, as Sharon Zukin notes in relation to postmodern urbanism more generally, 'a common cultural strategy that imposes a new way of seeing landscape: internationalizing it, abstracting a legible image from the service economy, connecting it to consumption rather than production' (Zukin 1996: 45). However, there are other ways of seeing Birmingham – some in tension with the visions of the commercial imagineers, some in concert with them – and this volume brings together practitioners and academics to represent and comment on the visual culture of urban regeneration as a key context for understanding the remaking of the city. *Remaking Birmingham* treats the city as a visual environment in which perception contributes profoundly to regeneration – many of the contributors explore the relationships between historical and contemporary ways of seeing and representing change in Birmingham. They consider how the design and building of the cityscape encode visual understandings of urban space; how the relationship between the built environment and social process is mediated by the visual forms of the city; how strategies for rebranding the city impact upon its broader visual economy; and how planners, architects, artists and image-makers participate in urban representation and redevelopment. They also address the need to visualize new ideas of place and community within post-industrial urbanism.

The focus on visual culture refers us to the importance of recognizing the significant role of urban arts and culture in producing and contesting the city's symbolic economy. This role has been complexly reconfigured in relation to urban regeneration in recent years. When Joseph Chamberlain promoted an urban renaissance in Birmingham in the late nineteenth century he could draw on a common belief of the time that 'architecture, art and design should provide visual expression for the philosophy of the civic gospel' (Hartnell 1995: 232). Today, though, there is no such consensus view of the social (and moral) role of the urban arts; indeed, it is questionable as to whether there is even a common visual language that would encourage diverse urban populations to identify a civic function for the arts. Yet, at the same time, culture is being increasingly integrated into the promotion of urban renaissance projects and redevelopment schemes, and into broader national and international urban programmes (such as the European Union's Capital of Culture competition).[4] This promotional role for culture can introduce creative tensions for artists and cultural producers, bringing into question the principles of socially engaged art and mystifying issues of aesthetic value and shared meaning (see Miles 2000). However, this promotional role rarely encapsulates even as it powerfully conditions urban creativity as a mode of regeneration. In Birmingham, as elsewhere, artists and cultural producers work with many mixed motivations and ideals in contributing to urban regeneration. There is certainly evidence of poverty of imagination and franchised creativity in the city, but also evidence of individuals and groupings of people working to use art to create new forms of cross-cultural communication, and rethink the meanings and values of community, creativity and citizenship. This volume presents some significant examples – Jubilee Arts and The Public project in West Bromwich, the Sozo Collective in Handsworth, and Creative Partnerships across Birmingham, to name only a few – all, in different ways, involved in rethinking and actively developing new ways to integrate art and cultural practices within the regeneration of urban fabrics and communities.

Visual culture, then, frames regeneration as the relationship between aesthetic, cultural and socio-economic practices. As such, it is not responsive to the idea(l) of a common visual language or cultural commonality. Nor should it be when Birmingham is the subject, for this is a city visually characterized by disjunction and incongruity, reflecting its complex mixes of urban forms and populations. Positioned, all-too-visibly, between decline and regeneration, the landscape of the city and its environs collages old and new, producing dramatic contrasts – of industrial and post-industrial urbanisms, of crumbling modernist brutalism and spectacular flagship developments, of Victorian housing and South Asian lifestyles – that compound the aesthetic and socio-economic meanings of regeneration. Some commentators have idealized the city's urban differences as a form of urban 'fusion' or 'synthesis' or 'hybridity'. This is not surprising, for Birmingham's 'lack' of identity is also an element of its civic and cultural strengths; the idea of fusion makes a virtue out of the admixture of mobile cultural practices that are diffusely rooted and routed in and beyond the city. This can be a fresh, progressive way of conceiving of Birmingham as a multicultural city, but it can also be a way of levelling differences into a glossy multiculturalism in which only certain fragments of the mix (most often, cuisine and music) are rendered visible, part of the symbolic economy. This said, though, fusion has become an inspiration for creative practice in the city (see architect Wendy Shillam's comments in this volume) and it may yet prove to be a signature ideal for a city with an uneven yet fascinating modern history of 'accommodating difference' (Plant 2003).

Birmingham offers a particularly rich example for visual study as it strives to build a new city image. *Remaking Birmingham* integrates multiple disciplinary frames of reference and critical perspective, including contributions from specialists in architecture, public and community arts, photography, film-making, and urban studies – their perspectives refer us to both practical and critical understandings of the relations between urban visual culture and regeneration.

The first section, 'Concrete Dreams', focuses on urban design and architecture, with varied perspectives on issues of public space, community and consultation. Joe Holyoak examines the planning and design history of the Bull Ring (the most recent development, retitled The BullRing, is the largest city centre retail-led development project in Europe) and addresses contextual issues of public space, local identity and community

I.5
Roofing of mosque, Lozells Road, Birmingham, 2003
Photo Vanley Burke

democracy. His claim that the new BullRing is not sustainable and diminishes the public sphere of the city is a challenge to the aims and values of city managers. Deborah Parsons provides a companion piece in her focus on the flagship building in the BullRing development, Future Systems' Selfridges' Building – she situates it historically in relation to early 'arcade' shopping experiences in Birmingham and speculates on the aesthetic appeal of Birmingham's brand new urbanity. Wendy Shillam moves us away from city centre projects to comment on the development of an architectural 'aesthetic' in Birmingham, influenced by cultural fusions and exemplified by recent projects her architectural practice has undertaken in Saltley and in Handsworth in the city. The projects have placed strong emphasis on consultation with local Asian communities to learn how people felt about notions of home, city, colour and design. Glenn Howells considers some of the pitfalls of seeking to design iconic buildings and asks that more careful attention is given to creating a coherent fabric of sustainable buildings in Birmingham. In contrast to this, Will Alsop criticizes the lack of risk in British urban planning and building and considers the merits of creating iconic buildings. He also talks candidly and passionately about local projects, including the redesign of New Street Station in Birmingham and The Public Building in West Bromwich, which he credits as a huge influence on his approach to community consultation.

In Part II, 'Interventions', the role of art and culture in urban regeneration is more directly addressed. Sylvia King vividly describes the history of Jubilee Arts (now The Public) and comments on ways in which it works to energize the cultural life of local communities, expanding ideas of what constitutes arts practice. As Chief Executive of The Public she has worked closely with Will Alsop in rethinking the role of creativity in urban regeneration. Tim Hall looks at the central role that public art has played in recent waves of urban regeneration. Focusing on recent projects in central Birmingham (and with emphasis on the ill-fated *Forward* statue – destroyed by fire in 2003), he examines the meanings, roles and functions of public art in this context, and also the ways in which it affects the public's experience of new or regenerated urban spaces. Deborah Kermode comments on the growing practice of galleries producing off-site art in urban contexts. The Ikon Gallery has been a leading example of this practice, generating debates about the relationship between art, artist and audience in public settings, and the author illustrates several Ikon projects. Graham Gussin and Nigel Prince collaborated on an off-site project commissioned by Ikon and based at Spaghetti Junction. *Merge* works to illuminate aesthetic and technological aspects of this iconic network of roads, defamiliarizing everyday and stereotypical perceptions of 'motor city' Birmingham. Dave Pollard blurs the boundaries of builder and artist in his creative 'interventions' in the built environment. Working with a collective of Birmingham and international artists he transformed a terrace of five derelict Victorian mansions in Handsworth into a temporary exhibition space. The exhibition was a striking fusion of arts practice and community development and held up a critical mirror (of memory) to the dynamics of creative destruction in Birmingham.

The third section, 'Imagineering Birmingham', illustrates and comments on various modes and mediums of visual representation that frame 'Birmingham'. Peter James introduces and analyses selections from the rich history of photographic surveys documenting urban change in the city since the 1880s. He focuses on issues of civic space and representation and considers the broader significance of the medium of photography in relation to cultural and economic regeneration. Justin Edgar explores some of the reasons why Birmingham has only obliquely registered in cinematic representation and illustrates several examples, bringing to visibility a barely acknowledged history of urban imagery. Jane Lutz, a member of the team that prepared Birmingham's bid for European Capital of Culture, comments on the mechanics and difficulties involved in the bidding process, and on the importance of promoting new visual images of the city. Vanley Burke approaches the 'image' of Birmingham very differently, providing a richly observed and textured photo-essay of distinct cultural communities in the city. The photographs work to suggest ways in which individuals and groups of people shape and are shaped by their urban environments. Maria Balshaw provides a coda for the volume, reflecting on a number of recurrent concerns and advancing fresh propositions about what it means to consider Birmingham a 'creative city'. In particular, she outlines a model of urban change that identifies the creative energies of the city in the disjunctions between residual and emergent cultures.

Perhaps due to its historical development as 'a working city created simply as a means to make things, rather than to reflect on its nature *as* a city' (Higgott 2000: 151), Birmingham has readily thrown itself into major redevelopment projects, yet lacked a confident or compelling sense of identity. In the midst of another major wave of regeneration, there is an opportunity to reflect on its *re*making as a twenty-first-century city. Of course, the commercial imagineers are already involved in intense reflection about the city's image, but too much of this reflection is PR-led. If, as Will

I.6
Signs of urban change, 2003

Alsop remarks, 'Birmingham was the future', then it needs to learn from the errors of past regenerations, not simply seek to erase them through rebuilding or image makeovers. The concrete dreams of the twentieth century made a prison house of urban reality for many of the city's inhabitants, and the legacies of those dreams are still being lived out today. *Remaking Birmingham* offers some timely critical reflections on the city now emerging from the ruins of the future.

Notes

1　Beryl Bainbridge reported her impressions of being a pedestrian in Birmingham during a brief visit in the summer of 1983: 'An elderly couple, clinging to each other, stood marooned on the pavement beneath the massive bulk of a multi-storey car park. They were trying to cross the road but they were on a corner and the traffic swept round and round without ceasing. We walked through an underground tunnel and onto escalators. There were hundreds of us, black, white, yellow, brown, a multifarious army riding up from the gates of hell to be spewed out into the heavenly halls of the shopping precinct' (Quoted in Hedges 1991: 40).

2　This resonant phrase was used as the title of photographer Tom Merilion's exhibition of aerial images of landmark modern buildings in Birmingham. See p. 105 in this volume.

3　The desire of entrepreneurs and city leaders to construct a fresh city image mimics the view of global city theorists that 'the particularity and identity of cities is about product differentiation; their cultures and traditions are now sustained through the discourses of marketing and advertising' (Robins 1994: 306).

4　Birmingham was a leading competitor for Capital of Culture 2008 and I write a few days after the announcement that the bid was won by Liverpool. Among the hasty post-mortem comments about the Birmingham bid are criticisms of the 'top-down' composition of the bid team's interpretation and presentation of the city's 'culture'. To be sure, their idea of 'culture' had limited appeal across the city's diverse communities and the failure of the bid reflected the limitations of PR-led imagineering in creating a compelling and inclusive urban identity. It also brought to the fore Birmingham's historical and perpetual 'lack' of identity, though Birmingham boosters have not been keen to acknowledge this.

Part I

Concrete Dreams

Chapter 1

Street, Subway and Mall

Spatial Politics in the Bull Ring

Joe Holyoak

The production, management and occupation of public urban space are political activities of the utmost importance to citizens. One wishes that to write this opening sentence were a platitudinous statement of the obvious, but sadly this is not the case. Too often, public urban space, if it is thought about at all, is thought of as neutral territory; merely the space left over between the buildings. Buildings – what urban designers call collectively the city's urban fabric – obviously contribute greatly to the forming of the city's character, its identity, its spirit. But while they may be beautiful or ugly or just ordinary, buildings possess little in the way of a political dimension, because little of the public life of the city takes place within them. Public life predominantly takes place outside, in the street and the square, in the public realm; *Life Between Buildings*, as a respected book on the subject describes it (Gehl 1996).

This inhabitation of public space is political, because it raises issues of ownership, of control, of complexity, of conflicts of use, of limits on freedom of activity, which affect the well-being of the individual and the community, and on which decisions have somehow to be made, whether consensually or not. These issues are generally not present in the interior of even the most public building. If I go to a concert in Symphony Hall in Birmingham, I am content that the programme is decided by someone else, that the start and finish times are fixed, and that between those times I occupy the seat allocated to me. But if upon leaving Symphony Hall, I find that what appeared yesterday to be a public square is now fenced off, and dedicated to a private commercial activity, say the launch of the new model of Rover car, then I experience a dispossession. Clearly, I was mistaken in thinking that, as a citizen, I had some right of occupation over this apparently public space, some freedom of choice and action.

This sense of diminishment of the public realm is a commonplace nowadays. It is typically caused by a political process whereby public space is metamorphosed into private space, or at best, quasi-public space. Centenary Square is a quasi-public space; it looks like a public square, but it is not. It is a City Council-owned private space that the public is allowed to use when it is not being used for something else. The privatization of public space is mostly associated with large urban retail redevelopments. Here we typically see the traditional, all-purpose public street being replaced by something more narrowly tailored to a single purpose which suits the developer's interests; a 'retail environment'. The saga of the arguments over the redevelopment of the Bull Ring is the most prominent case in Birmingham where the political nature of public space has been made explicit, and become the focus of public debate.[1]

The Bull Ring is where the markets of Birmingham have been situated since a royal charter allowing a market was granted in 1166 to what was then a small village. In most towns the market square, which in Birmingham followed a typical English pattern of the widening out of the High Street into a triangular space, closed by the parish church at the far end, has usually been the central public space. This reflects the dominant role of mercantile exchange in its life and culture. In Birmingham the open air market of the Bull Ring drew around itself a supportive network of other traders, inns and businesses, and eventually the town's first major nineteenth-century public building, the Market Hall. But during the nineteenth century the centre of the town migrated westwards, and the Bull Ring was no longer the central public space. A more bourgeois, cultural and administrative centre grew around the new focal spaces of Victoria Square and Chamberlain Place. This emphasized by contrast the role of the Bull Ring as the city's working-class locus. Today, with the growth of other shopping alternatives for the more affluent and mobile, the markets are economically important for the elderly and for poorer working-class families in particular.

Until 1959, the Bull Ring (shown in Figure 1.1) was a popular, democratic, public space. It was not particularly attractive, but it was a vigorous, lively, sensually rich public realm; vulgar in the best sense of the word. Market traders and shops were joined by salesmen, hawkers, the noted escapologist and other performers. It was a public arena that was open to possibilities, a theatre of spontaneous popular culture. Topographically the Bull Ring was made memorable by its gradient; the space fell about 15 metres from New Street down to the parish church, rendering it even more theatrical.

1.1
The Bull Ring in 1952

1.2
The Bull Ring in 1970

Then modernist replanning arrived with the simultaneous building of the Inner Ring Road (the Queensway) and the Bull Ring Centre, Britain's first city-centre indoor shopping mall. Together, these two developments destroyed the coherence of the urban space of the Bull Ring. Remarkably the outdoor market stayed more or less where it previously had been. But instead of occupying a legible urban square, connected to adjacent places by conventional streets, the market (shown in Figure 1.2) was hemmed in between and underneath highways, reached only by unpleasant and disorientating subways and passages. The Bull Ring Centre itself, built by Laing Developments, was a disastrous failure in both design and economic terms.[2]

The redevelopment of the Bull Ring by Hammerson, which will be completed in 2003, will create the third environment in this place during my lifetime and those of my contemporaries. It began with the purchase in the mid-1980s of the remainder of Laing's lease by the developers London and Edinburgh Trust (LET), which was followed by years of public argument over the correct form for a new development. It was an opportunity to identify the fundamental mistakes made in the development of the 1963 Bull Ring Centre, under the influence of misguided modernist doctrine, and to revert to what by that time was established as an orthodox postmodern urban design strategy.

This strategy was proposed by the campaigning group Birmingham for People, of which the author was a member during its existence from 1988 to 1998, in its 1989 alternative development proposal called *The People's Plan for the Bull Ring* (Birmingham for People 1989) which can be seen in Figures 1.3–1.6. Its constituent elements can be summarized as

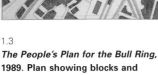

1.3
The People's Plan for the Bull Ring, 1989. Plan showing blocks and streets

1.4
The People's Plan for the Bull Ring, 1989. Perspective view of the new marketplace, looking towards St Martin's

follows: a mixture of land uses, the shaping of a traditional marketplace enclosed by buildings, medium-sized blocks of buildings, conventional outdoor streets, and all pedestrian and vehicular movement at ground level. These elements were all traditional, not to say old-fashioned, which meant that in the context of 1989 *The People's Plan* was surprisingly radical.

These urban elements are in opposition to what retail developers generally want to build. The purest form of the developers' retail model can be seen in out-of-town developments such as Meadowhall near Sheffield, or Bluewater in Kent. Here, instead of mixed uses, there is retail use only, with perhaps some 'leisure' uses added to enrich the shopping experience. Instead of a fine grain of urban blocks such as we find in a conventional city centre, there is gargantuan scale; what in architectural terms we might call the megastructural approach. Instead of outdoor streets and squares, there are indoor malls. And of course, and most critically, these indoor malls are not public spaces; they are privately owned space, and they have doors that close at the end of shopping hours.

The choice of the private, indoor mall as the preferred form for new retail development represents a fear, or at least distrust, of the street. The public space of the street is an arena for the unpredictable. Not only might rain fall on your head, but you might encounter strange people, poor people, ugly people, there for a variety of different purposes, exhibiting a variety of different kinds of behaviour. All over that part of the world where the traditional street was degraded in the mid-twentieth century by the dominance of modernism, the social and sensory stimulation of the public street is being rediscovered and celebrated. This is truer in Birmingham than in most places. Contemporary with the development of the 1963 Bull Ring Centre, streets all over the city centre and beyond were reduced to mere

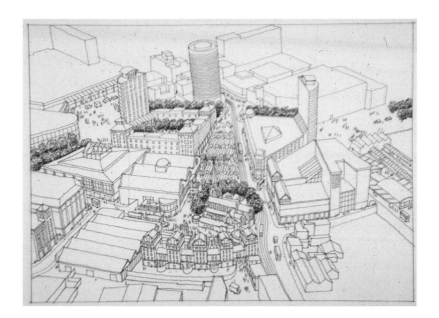

1.5
The People's Plan for the Bull Ring,
**1989. Aerial perspective, looking
towards the city centre**

1.6
The People's Plan for the Bull Ring,
**1989. Model of the proposed
development**

utilitarian corridors for vehicles, with pedestrians consigned to subways. The renaissance of public space in Birmingham in recent years – the pedestrianization of New Street, the redesign of Victoria Square, the creation of Centenary Square and Brindleyplace Square – has been a great popular success, and has been recognized by several official awards.

In these places, the true nature and purpose of the street as a sociable space, which has been true everywhere for millennia, are once again acknowledged. Among the wide range of examples of humankind that may be encountered there may be some which are strange, or unpleasant, or even threatening. Yet the fundamental principle that Jane Jacobs documented as long ago as 1961 is still self-evidently true: a well-used and well-populated street is a safe street, as well as a stimulating street (Jacobs 1961). In Birmingham we may now see citizens strolling the streets and squares purely for pleasure, in a version of the Italian *passeggiata* – something unheard of 20 years ago.[3]

The nineteenth-century shopping arcade, such as Great Western Arcade or City Arcade in Birmingham, was an *addition* to the network of traditional streets. They were typically cut through existing urban blocks to create additional retail frontage, getting more out of a given area. They were indeed usually private spaces, and were gated after shop opening hours. But their closure at night did not reduce the utility of the street network; they augmented it when they were open.

The threat of the modern urban retail development, by contrast, is that, through distrust or fear of the street, it seeks to replace the public street with the private mall. The initial 1987 design for the redevelopment of the Bull Ring, by the architects Chapman Taylor for LET (shown in Figure 1.7), proposed a giant box containing three levels of indoor mall, 500 metres in length. This was what *The People's Plan* set out to counter. Entirely introverted, it had no positive connection with streets, and would have been extremely disruptive to the existing street network (already damaged by the 1960s' redevelopment and roadbuilding). In 1988, its architect described the proposal as 'a huge aircraft-carrier settled on the streetscape of the city'.[4] He presumably thought this an admirable vision – others were understandably horrified by the prospect.

Over the past 50 years, we have seen three different models for how a city centre might be organized, one rapidly succeeding another. We might call them Street City, Subway City, and Mall City. The first, very ancient, was a city centre made of a series of outward-facing blocks of buildings, set in a continuous network of streets shared by pedestrians and vehicles, as in Figure 1.8. This was the pattern that the radical architect

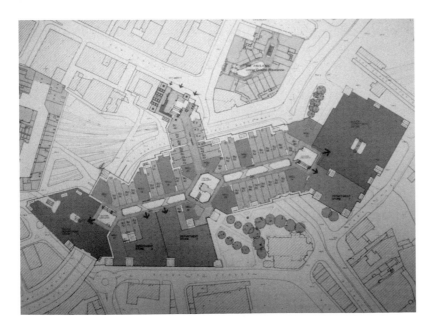

1.7
Mall-level plan of the original LET proposal for The Galleries, 1987

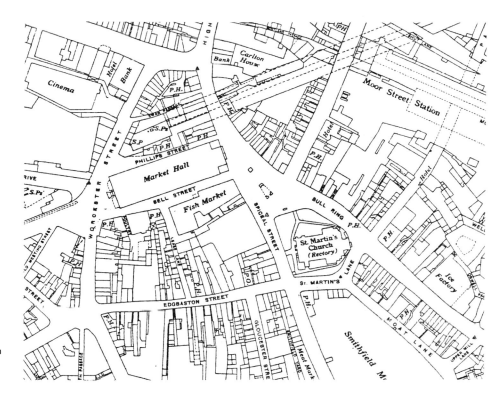

1.8

Street city: the Ordnance Survey plan of the Bull Ring in 1938

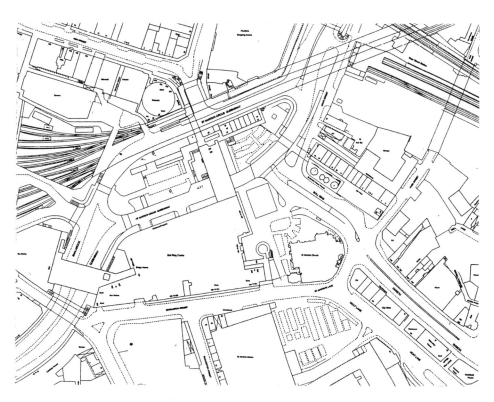

1.9

Subway city: the Ordnance Survey plan of the Bull Ring in 1990, following the development of the Bull Ring Centre and the Inner Ring Road

and town-planner Le Corbusier wished to consign to the dustbin of history in 1933. 'Our streets no longer work. Streets are an obsolete notion. There ought not to be such things as streets; we have to create something that will replace them' (Le Corbusier 1967).

Under the influence of Le Corbusier and his European allies, Street City was replaced by a model in which vehicles and pedestrians were, as far as possible, separated, as in Figure 1.9 – Subway City. In line with the modernist rhetoric, the physical and psychological disruption caused by the transformation was actually seen by its promoters as a cause for pride. A 1959 article about 'The New Birmingham' in the *Birmingham Mail* by the powerful chairman of the Public Works Committee, Alderman Frank Price, bragged 'Could you find your way around this city centre?' (Price 1959).

The answer from the subway was, unsurprisingly, 'no!', or perhaps, 'yes, but with great difficulty!' (Goodey *et al.*1971). The pedestrian subway was public space, but so dysfunctional and squalid it was not worthy of the name. It did not take long to realize that the replacement of the humane, legible, but untidy Street City by a model in which engineering gave priority to vehicles produced an environment that was unpleasant, unsafe, disorientating, and which, as the Bull Ring Centre dramatically demonstrated, did not even work economically (see Marriott 1967). But it took longer to gather the nerve to admit the mistake and to do something about it. The response by an alliance of planners and retail developers, this time influenced by the USA rather than Europe, was to build the privileged private indoor mall, and to leave the unpleasantness outside.

The first version of The Galleries, as LET's new Bull Ring was to be called, and the subsequent modifications of it, exemplified the third model of Mall City. At the 1988 Highbury Conference on the planning of the city centre, the chairman of the Planning Committee, Councillor Fred Chapman, not realizing he was transparently giving the game away, proudly described The Galleries as 'the largest out-of-town shopping centre in a city centre'.[5] The campaign against the LET proposals, over several years, by Birmingham for People succeeded in moderating this alien invasion considerably. The single, gigantic block became split into two smaller (but still large) parts; an outdoor pedestrian space approximating to the size of the pre-Bull Ring Centre market square was inserted, and the proportion of shops on indoor malls was reduced.

The greatest single achievement won by *The People's Plan* was the closure of the section of the Queensway at St Martin's Circus. The arrival of the Inner Ring Road in the early 1960s is a classic example of severance, the enforced separation of parts of the city, both physically and perceptually. Before this happened, the Bull Ring was part of the city centre; one simply walked down the hill from New Street and High Street into the markets. The Inner Ring Road at a stroke put the markets outside the city centre, connected to it only by a miserable subway. Birmingham for People proposed retrieving the premodernist situation by closing the Queensway between

New Street Station and Moor Street Station, linking them by a bus- and taxi-only road, which pedestrians could cross easily at surface level.

Councillor Chapman, the director of LET, John Newman, and his architect all lined up to proclaim this bold proposal 'a fantasy'. 'No one in his wildest dreams could imagine the ring road being stopped up,' said Newman.[6] A little over a year later it was part of City Council policy, and incorporated into the latest revision of The Galleries plan. On the other hand, the part of *The People's Plan* which had no effect at all was the proposal for a mixed use development, as opposed to totally retail, which LET were proposing, and Hammerson are building. This was despite a recently adopted City Council policy that all large new developments should have a mixture of uses. Most critical in the view of Birmingham for People was the inclusion of residential use. This was some years before the huge building boom of upmarket apartments in the west and north of the city centre. Referring to the city centre, John Newman asked dismissively, 'But who wants to live there? Would you?' – a rhetorical question that rates highly on the scale of myopia.[7]

Since Hammerson purchased the site from LET in 1996, with the planning permission that LET had eventually secured, after years of struggle, some of the hard-won elements of the public realm have unfortunately been lost. We no longer have the ground-level pedestrian connection between High Street and the Bull Ring. Instead, the route bridges over the top of the new bus and taxi-only road. As in the 1963 Bull Ring Centre scheme, the natural topography of the location is being distorted by engineering. Instead of walking down into the Bull Ring, we begin by walking *up*. Critically, the legibility of this part of the city is damaged as a consequence; from High Street we see only the upper part of St Martin's Church, and nothing of the space that lies around it.

In addition, the proportion of private indoor malls to public outdoor spaces in the development (shown in Figure 1.10) has increased from the approved LET scheme. Developers and their managers prefer the indoor mall to the street because they can replace common law, which governs people's use of the street, with a set of rules that suits their own interests. If they wish, they can exclude dogs, casual eating, standing about talking, and any activity which they judge to be incompatible with the retailing experience. Needless to say, any kind of demonstration, or even the selling of *The Big Issue*, will not take place in Mall City.

The democracy of the street allows an urban society to be what it is, and to show what it is, for better or worse. In the mall we see a deliberately engineered social and environmental uniformity, one that does not reflect the richness and complexity of real life. I am reminded of the remark that a security officer in the Meadowhall shopping centre made to me, after he had spoken to a group of young men. 'They were swearing. We've got some nice people here and they don't want to hear that kind of language' (Holyoak 1990). Architects' perspectives of the proposed malls faithfully

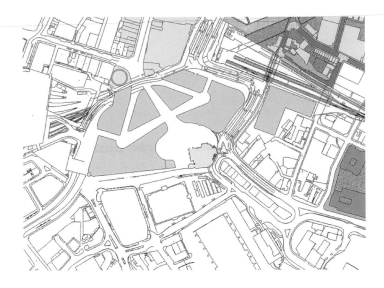

1.10
Mall city: the plan of the Hammerson development of the BullRing, 2003

represent the desired product of the social engineering: uniformly happy, prosperous and conventionally attractive people, dedicated only to consuming. To the injury done to the history of urban space is added the insult of the name. The historic name of the Bull Ring, which until recently was the name of a public street which had existed for centuries, even surviving the 1960s' cataclysm, has been appropriated by Hammerson as their private property, and converted into BullRing. It is now a brand, the name of a piece of private property. The privatization of the name, following the privatization of urban space, has apparently been accepted by the City Council without a murmur of protest.

On the north side of St Martin's Church, there is to be a large space, to be known as St Martin's Square. This had been the location of the outdoor markets for centuries, until their recent exile to the distant side of the church and Edgbaston Street. In towns and cities all over the world, the outdoor market is the *raison d'être* for the urban space, giving it purpose, identity and animation. But here the market has been banished. This of course is not a true public space, but another quasi-public space, owned and managed by Hammerson. Although outdoor, it will apparently be managed as if it were an indoor mall. At the time of writing (2003), publicity notices tell us: 'A full and exciting programme of events and activities are planned for the square, to entertain you and your family during the day but also after hours'. The organic, democratic spontaneity of urban society, which has generated and animated urban space since the time of the ancient Greeks, is evidently not to be trusted.[8]

From the earliest LET proposals for the Bull Ring in the 1980s, there has appeared to be a perception in the minds of the developers that a new shopping centre and the markets could not intimately coexist. Although no one has ever gone on record on this matter, what is being built expresses very clearly a policy of class-based *apartheid*, separating the middle-class shopping centre from the predominantly working-class markets. This appears to be a particularly British kind of snobbery. Certainly one would not find a similar perception being expressed in Milan, or even in patrician Turin, where different classes of businesses and customers share a common respectability, and share the common territory of the city.

Following 15 years of argument about the form of the new Bull Ring, Birmingham's market traders have ended up with a poor deal. In the realpolitik contest for space, they have lost out to the greater power of the retail developers. They have ceded their historic location to the north of St Martin's Church to the shopping centre, and retreated further away down-hill from the city core, south of Edgbaston Street. On the positive side, all of the different markets, indoor and outdoor, are now contiguous, but they are now more peripheral to the city.

When the first LET proposal for redevelopment, the 'aircraft carrier', was published in 1987, the market traders were the first to organize in opposition to it. They correctly realized that their livelihoods were threatened by it. The Hammerson scheme now being built does not wall off the markets from the city core, as that original scheme proposed, and is more permeable. But the markets are still disadvantaged. One suspects that if the market traders had conducted an organized, committed and open campaign against the mall-centred proposals, they would have generated a huge wave of public opinion in their support. But their opposition was always compromised by the knowledge that the City Council is their landlord, and their consequent fear of the possible economic consequences of being too outspoken. The community and the public realm are poorer as a result.

The public realm is where we become citizens. In the street, in the square, or in the market, we are citizens; in the mall, we are consumers. With the privatization of public space, with the replacement of the public street by the private mall, the arena of citizenship is reduced in size. The influence of commercial interests increases, even over public space that still remains public. In Birmingham, the City Centre Manager is answerable to an unelected board that is dominated by retail and business interests. The latest British city centre management idea, again under American influence, is the Business Improvement District (BID).[9] Within the BID, public control of the management of the public street is traded in exchange for funding from the business sector.

The privatization of public urban space is part of a wider political pattern, of the reduction of the public sphere of the nation. This programme was introduced by the Thatcher governments in the 1980s, and is now being even more vigorously expanded under New Labour. The idea of common ownership – of space, of the means of supply, of health and educational institutions – and the idea that these embody and represent the community, whether at a municipal or a national level, has been devalued. New buildings for schools and hospitals are delivered by the private sector, through the Private Finance Initiative, as business products. The schools, colleges and hospitals themselves are increasingly run as autonomous businesses by technocratic and commercial interests, outside the democratic remit of the community.

The BullRing is a small, local illustration of this phenomenon. It will be a splendid shopping centre. But it is too inflexible, too monocultural, too narrowly defined, too contained within its own boundaries, to be an effective part of a city centre, which is a rather more complex kind of creature. In this, its makers are repeating the fundamental mistakes made by Laing in the 1960s, but this time on a bigger scale. The urban model of medium-scale blocks and streets has shown itself to be a sustainable form, capable of surviving and prospering, through incremental adjustments, for hundreds of years. The model of the giant internalized mall is not sustainable. I expect the new BullRing to have a rate of obsolescence similar to the Bull Ring Centre which it replaced – leading to demolition in about, let's say, 2040.

Notes

1 A more detailed account of the Birmingham for People campaign can be found in Holyoak (2002).
2 An excellent account of the reasons for failure is given in Marriott (1967).
3 To refer to the *passeggiata* is a reminder that the covered street has an honourable role in the history of public space. We have the grandparents of the western urban arcade in the 1850s' *galleria* of Milan and Naples, and further east, many wonderful examples of *bazaar*, the linear covered market, can be found in cities such as Cairo and Isfahan. These spaces have roofs, and human behaviour within is therefore subtly modified, but they are still public streets, like their outdoor neighbours.
4 Reported in *The Birmingham Post*, 10 March 1988.
5 Reported by Martin Spring, *Building,* 8 April 1988.
6 Reported in *The Birmingham Post*, 23 August 1989 and 24 November 1989, and Rodney Carran, the *Observer,* 3 December 1989.
7 Reported by Jonathan Glancey, the *Independent*, 11 October 1989.
8 For an excellent account of the American practice, which is being imported here, see Sorkin (1992).
9 At the time of writing (2003) a study is being made for the creation of a BID in Birmingham city centre.

Chapter 2

Shopping for the Future

The Re-enchantment of Birmingham's Urban Space

Deborah Parsons

> In the centre of Fedora, that grey stone metropolis, stands a metal building with a crystal globe in every room. Looking into each globe, you see a blue city, the model of a different Fedora. These are the forms the city could have taken if, for one reason or another, it had not become what we see today.
>
> (Calvino 1974: 34)

Birmingham entered the new millennium with a great gash at its centre, a crater of ochre earth and rubble; gaping, raw, expectant. Weekend crowds, ushered along temporary walkways on their way to the markets inconveniently located on the other side of the cavernous expanse, paused mid-purpose to watch the demolition of the past and to wonder at the possibilities of the future. The most prescient were taking photographs, producing week-after-week records of a city in transition. Young children were hoisted on shoulders, to peer through the wire grating down onto the adult Lego below. Elderly couples contemplated suddenly reinforced memories.

Over a year later a veiled shape has slowly arisen from the dust and mud, to stand amidst the Victorian brick and post-war concrete that is Birmingham's architectural heritage. Approaching the city by train, you are at present greeted by the playful contrast made by its polka-dot wrapping against the horizontal rings of the Rotunda rising behind. Architects Future Systems' design for the new Selfridges store in Birmingham was inspired by at once the skin of a chameleon and the sequins of a Paco Rabanne dress. Its curvaceous shape clad in a flexible sheath of polished aluminium discs, which will seem to give the exterior changing colour and texture, the building celebrates fashion and mutability in a space long notorious for a lack of beauty and a lot of concrete. As a surge of regeneration and renewal culminates in a massive cultural redevelopment scheme, and the arrival of the signature architects of British urban revival, Birmingham is shaking off its reputation as 'the ugliest city centre in the country' (Rogers and Power 2000: 279). Selfridges, with its voluptuous shape and shimmering façade, promises to flaunt the city's new image. Looking into its reflecting mirror, Birmingham preens and feels flattered.

How to approach the commodification and commercialization of public space as a common feature of contemporary urban planning is a thorny issue, as the field of urban studies repeatedly testifies (Shields 1992; Zukin 1988). Yet it is not an exclusively contemporary one. The current collaboration of architecture and the spaces and culture of consumption as a key force within urban regeneration is nothing new, and is indeed a dominant characteristic of the development of capitalist modernity in the late nineteenth and early twentieth centuries. This essay explores the role of a changing geography of consumption in the formations and perceptions of Birmingham at three distinctive moments in the city's spatial history; Joseph Chamberlain's master plan for its Victorian core, the concrete jungle that

2.1
Selfridges Building, Birmingham, 2003

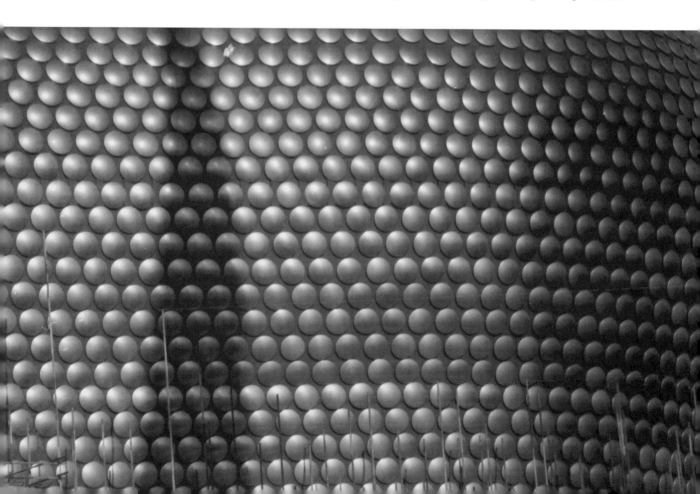

sacrificed the pedestrian to the car in the 1950s and 1960s, and, specifically, the embrace of a gentrified public urbanity that guides its contemporary regeneration. Social and historical studies of Birmingham have typically tended to concentrate on the city's industrial heritage, or to present a localized ethnography with a strong whiff of commercial nostalgia. Constant reinvention, however, is one of the historical characteristics of a city that has long been quick to demolish the past in favour of an embrace of the new. Here, I examine Birmingham's self-conscious transformation into a city of cosmopolitan urbanity, in terms of the spatial images and spatial patterns of display and consumption that make up its new urban space.

Window Shopping

It was not until the last quarter of the nineteenth-century, and the implementation of Joseph Chamberlain's 1875 Improvement Scheme, that Birmingham developed a notably modern retail culture. Chamberlain's vision followed the principles, if not the scale, of Baron Haussmann's Paris, and he approached the task with similar bullishness, clearing 93 acres of slum housing and impoverished streets, and displacing an estimated 16,000 people (Upton 1993: 155), for the creation of a modern metropolis. Cutting through the heart of this new topography was the elegant sloping avenue of Corporation Street, which, along with a renovated and embellished New Street, was to form an ideal site for commercial speculation. Eager for a purpose built department store to grace the city with its architectural grandeur, it was reportedly Chamberlain himself who invited David Lewis, the retail entrepreneur who had established his first store, the Bon Marché, in Liverpool in the 1870s, and already branched out to a second in Manchester in 1877, to take a prime location on the developing Corporation Street.[1] Lewis's was a company that catered for a broadly middle-class clientele, emphasizing quality for money and low profit margins over indulgence or luxury. Nevertheless, with its imposing if unelaborate exterior, gas lighting, grand double staircase rising from the ground to first floors, and ornamental lift, the Birmingham store, designed by H. R. Yeoville Thomason, the architect of the recent Council House and Art Gallery, epitomized spectacular and technological modernity. Its opening in September 1885, attended by an estimated 40,000 people, was described by the *Birmingham Daily Post* as 'an event rather of public than of private or business significance' (Briggs 1956: 87).

Perhaps the most striking feature of Birmingham's late nineteenth-century consumer landscape, however, was its flush of ornamental arcades, including the Great Western Arcade in 1876, the Central Arcade and Imperial Arcade in 1883, and the Colonnade Passage and the City Arcade in 1897, all linking the two boulevards with smaller streets in the city centre (Upton 1993: 185).[2] With their spectacular iron and glass structures and gas-lit chandeliers, arcades acted as illuminated streets that yet offered protection

2.2
Great Western Arcade exterior,
c. **1890s**

from both traffic and the elements. According to Frankfurt School theorist Walter Benjamin, the phenomenon of the arcade as it developed in 1820s' Paris thus created a perfect habitat for a culture of leisured urbanity, miniature cities in their own right, in which the dallying window-shopper or *flâneur* could linger before the multiple, marvellous commodities on display. 'Strolling could hardly have assumed the importance it did without the arcades' he declares (Benjamin 1973: 36).

The arcades can be seen as the forerunners of both the department store and the shopping mall. In Birmingham, as elsewhere, the decline of the former occurred concurrently with the development of the latter. Marshall and Snelgrove, which had opened on New Street in 1926, closed in 1969, followed by the city's oldest store, the Beehive Warehouse, in 1972, the Co-Op, which made way for the Pavilions shopping mall in 1987, and finally Lewis's itself four years later. The mall, although separated from the city, was also an attempt to stand in for it, an enclosed utopian environment that provided the facilities of the city without the chaos and disorder of its everyday street life.

The Bull Ring Centre in Birmingham led the way for the British mall. In direct response to the 1963 Buchanan Report privileging traffic access to city centres, it turned its back on the street and, encased within its self-contained precinct, ultimately the city itself. The old-style department stores had presented a diversity of goods to the consumer, but in their provision of luxurious services and relaxation facilities intended to enhance the shopping experience, they also acted crucially as spaces of sociability, theatricality and entertainment. By contrast the drab, faceless, predictable mall offered none of the 'cityness' of the city. Now, after two decades in which the mall has become an object of sustained critique across Europe, sweeping policy change by urban government has embraced a vision of public urbanity as key to the enhancement of a marketable environment. In the urban design framework of *The Birmingham Plan* (Birmingham City Council 1993), and the Birmingham Marketing Partnership's recent campaign, 'Birmingham – A New Heart, A New Spirit' (2001), the Bull Ring is to be restored as the city's central node, a public meeting place for sociable consumption.

Pedestrian or *Flâneur*?

'But is it possible to *flân* in Birmingham?', a colleague asked me recently, with some incredulity. According to recent marketing, the city that so worshipped the car that it incarcerated itself within the 'concrete collar' of the inner ring road, is now a city for strolling. The Brummie *flâneur* (a tautological concept less than a decade ago) can amble aimlessly from Brindleyplace through Centenary Square to Chamberlain's pedestrianized boulevards, or along the canal at Gas Street Basin to the Mailbox, where the unsuspected delight of a balloon-lit underpass then acts as a second, fantasy gateway to New Street station and the Victorian city centre. Or at least he can in Birmingham's newly idealized vision of itself. *Flânerie* in its popular contemporary form, characterized by a nonchalant and leisured sauntering of city streets, does not come naturally to the British urban citizen, attuned to a less than auspicious climate, and for whom the ubiquitous presence of CCTV merely confirms an innate self-consciousness and suspicion towards purposeless drifting. Nevertheless, loitering with the intent to consume is an acceptable, even *de rigueur*, aspect of contemporary, gentrified city living – and why use such mundane terms as 'pedestrianism', when '*flânerie*' sounds so much more seductive and cosmopolitan?

'City living' has become an ever-present slogan across Birmingham's city centre, in which every warehouse redevelopment or new building project provides further balconied penthouses and studio apartments for a style-hungry clientele. The twenty-something interviewees of the imaginatively titled lifestyle magazine, *City Living* – for example, typically media executives, restaurant managers, designers or DJs – ooze enthusiasm for Birmingham's new-found cosmopolitanism as they perch on neutral leather amidst minimalist chrome and laminate interiors. Only occasionally, glimpsed through a window or from a balcony, does the unpredictability of a city street break into the carefully designed harmony. Advertised as 'The only magazine about Birmingham, for Birmingham', *City Living* presents a carefully pruned urban map, stretching from the new developments at Brindleyplace and the Mailbox, to the gentrified apartment blocks of the city centre and the Jewellery Quarter. The smug rhetoric of contemporary urban marketing risks making all but the city's upmarket scene invisible, naturalizing the commercialization of its public space. In this version of urban life, *flânerie* means merely the joys of well-heeled leisure.

Beyond the Public Relations speak, however, the transformation of spaces, buildings and infrastructure has altered the physiognomy of Birmingham, and the renewed supremacy of the pedestrian is symbolic of a shift in the way in which the city is starting to look at itself. The shaping of the city's new urban space, and the aestheticizing of its newly urbane identity, are perhaps most succinctly articulated in the work of artist Reuben Colley. In a series of paintings first exhibited at the Halcyon Gallery in November 2001 under the title 'Impressions of Birmingham', Colley becomes the city's own 'painter of modern life', recording its metamorphosis from a landscape of grey anonymity to a series of sites and sights of glamorous leisure and consumption. Several of his huge canvases commemorate the familiar concrete Birmingham of the 1960s, the inner ring road silently forlorn, devoid of people but also the vehicular traffic that it was built to satisfy. Yet if paintings such as *Traffic* recall a perception of the city that it is eager to discard, Colley's principal theme is the changing landscape and iconic leisure spaces of a new Birmingham. In *Skyline*, for example, depicting the rubble of the demolished Bull Ring, it is not the infamous Rotunda that dominates the scene but rather the crane placed in the foreground of the picture, thus seeming to tower over the landmark of a past era, a symbol of change within a city in transition. (See colour plate 2) A crane appears again at the edge of another large-scale work, showing Birmingham's canal side redevelopment as seen from new restaurant Santa Fe, again emphasizing the process of construction and change that has transformed the murky scene of the canals at night with luminous turquoise neon.

Despite the vibrancy of colour that characterizes the night-time scenes of Birmingham's new urban space, and the spectacle with which cultural and consumer regeneration is shown to endow the city landscape, these early images by Colley also evoke a sense of detachment from their principal subject. The bars and restaurants of contemporary Birmingham, for example, (Santa Fe, Petit Blanc, Bank) are typically depicted from the outside, their patrons only indistinct figures within brightly-lit interiors. The Mailbox too, a vacant Royal Mail sorting office transformed into a multi-use complex of designer stores, restaurants, apartments and hotels, a scarlet beacon of gentrification shining in the night, appears to the observer as an enchanted but also unreal space. (See colour plate 3) The viewer in these scenes is encouraged to delight in the spectacle of the city, whilst at the same time separated from interaction with the luxuries it promises. Even in the daytime scenes of public spaces such as Victoria or Centenary Square, people become little more than shadowy passers-by. The artist remains throughout a detached observer, the *flâneur*, who in his many guises from rag-picker to leisured consumer marvels at the ephemeral beauty of the urban moment, 'addicted to its optical illusions' (Gilloch 2002: 132). Colley undoubtedly paints to his market, such works representing the city in the image of its urban and urbane middle classes, but he also prompts recognition of the role of image and myth in the enchantments of a new Birmingham.

Urban Bazaar

For Walter Benjamin the architecture of consumption reveals the mythologies of its contemporary space and time. The nineteenth-century arcades, for example, lined with luxury boutiques for the leisured elite, epitomized for him both the phantasmagoria of modernity and, in their decline, a spatial disenchantment with its illusions. Dutch architect Rem Koolhaas is similarly, if more acerbically, both critical of and fascinated by the lustre and the debris of the contemporary architecture of consumption, what he describes as the 'junkspace' of the mall, architectural minimalism, the interchangeable brands of bland (Koolhaas 2001: 408). With the recent appearance of a new generation of 'cathedrals of consumption' (Crossick and Jaumaln 1999), however, the twenty-first century is witnessing a spatial 're-enchantment' (Shields 1992) of contemporary city centres. In Birmingham a rejection of architectural banality and a new interest in aesthetic retail design can in part be witnessed in the restored Great Western and Piccadilly Arcades, with their mock heritage décor, modish boutiques and curiosity shops, although it is in the Mailbox complex that we find a postmodern take on the arcade for the contemporary dandy – and in the forgotten shell of the City Arcade a reminder of the architecture of consumption's ephemeral magic.

Under the guidance of its zealous managing director Vittorio Radice, however, it is Selfridges that is leading the revitalization of the spectacular tradition in urban consumption in the UK. Taking up the legacy of the store's illustrious and showy founder, Radice wants Selfridges to be 'the best and most exciting department store chain in Europe by meeting the needs of [its] customers in a unique and theatrical way'.[3] This has meant a return to Gordon Selfridge's original marketing strategy and the vision of a store that 'will attract visitors for far more than shopping'. When Anna Levete of Future Systems, for example, emphasizes 'the social function such a building now plays in our society, as a meeting place, a place of entertainment, a place to browse, a marketplace', she calls to mind consumer architecture's previous golden age.[4] Yet beyond Radice's aspirations for a revival of the social and entertaining role of the department store, the 250,000 square foot Birmingham store is taking on an additional symbolic presence, intended to act as an icon of the new Birmingham and a catalyst for the further

2.3
Great Western Arcade, Birmingham, 2002

2.4
The Mailbox, Birmingham, 2003

regeneration of the Digbeth and East Side areas. If much of the new Bull Ring is being formed by the familiar style of atriumed retail and eating complex that is exchangeable with any number of other urban redevelopment schemes, Selfridges will be a landmark in its own right, signifying both store and city.

The gaping hole that was the Bull Ring a year ago, however, was by no means empty of meaning, a blank slate waiting for a building to be erected that would reinscribe it. And although change is itself historically embedded in Birmingham's cultural identity, its industrial and civic roots based in progress and innovation, the city is cautious not to once more simply throw away its past. 'No space disappears in the course of growth and development', Henri Lefebvre declares (Lefebvre 1991: 86). Every new urban plan adds only the most recent surface to the palimpsest of spatial affect. The Bull Ring has been the commercial heart of Birmingham since the twelfth century, a status that the much-maligned 1960s' Bull Ring Shopping Centre was at least intended to maintain, and that the current multi-million regeneration project at once commemorates and re-establishes. Moreover, in taking its place between St Martin's Church and the infamous

2.5
Interior of Selfridges Building, Birmingham, 2003

Rotunda, two previous landmarks of a city in transition, the Selfridges building will configure and complete a central vista for the new city that marks its past, present and future.

Haussmanization, the car-city of Spaghetti Junction and the Inner Ring Road, city living with its 'pacification by cappuccino'; is the Selfridges building simply the latest of Birmingham's attempts to jump on the bandwagon of urban regeneration, this time the signature building that promises a little of the 'Bilbao-effect'? Perhaps. The remaking of Birmingham depends not only on its built form or its symbolic representation, but on how these interact with the everyday practices and self-fashionings of its users. In the meantime Future Systems' sequinned department store glitters enticingly, promising a 'new look' for shopper and city alike.

Notes

1   Lewis's remained a provincial chain until its acquisition of Selfridges in London in 1951. Its Birmingham store closed in 1991, exactly a decade before, in an ironic reversal of fortune, a revitalized Selfridges under the leadership of Vittorio Radice began to expand with spectacular regional stores; first to Manchester in 2001, followed by Birmingham in 2002–3.
2   Sections of the Great Western and City arcades are still in existence, the former renovated in 1984 in accordance with its original Victorian decoration. One entrance to the Central Arcade can still be seen on Cannon Street.
3   'Selfridges Birmingham', Selfridges press pack, p. 2.
4   Interview with the author, 3 October 2002.

had been taken over by one of the Islamic groups, as a mosque. But perhaps that is not surprising when you see its fine tower – almost a minaret – and you examine the decorations, which plunder as much from Oriental influences as they do from the gothic or the classical. Birmingham's Victorian splendour was created on the backs of the empire.

People flocked to Birmingham in the post-war period to find work and a major influx of ethnic minorities can be traced back to these times. Many people we met had come to the city in the 1960s to work in the car and motorcycle industries – Saltley and Small Heath is just on the border of a vast swathe of industrial land – though by the 1970s these industries were becoming moribund. However, Birmingham was not aesthetically or culturally comfortable with its new ethnic mix. We were dismayed to see how modern architects had responded. We found that they were unable to respond to the cultural mingling with anything like the sophistication of their Victorian forebears. Modern buildings in the area tended to be cheap red brick, with garishly coloured ogee-arched windows – a style we soon dubbed 'Barratt's Mosque'.

3.1
The mosque on Coventry Road, Small Heath, Birmingham, 2002

Fusion

However, these schizophrenic buildings – neither western nor eastern – were displaying a cultural trend that we found all over Birmingham that was not restricted to architecture. By 1991, 21.5 per cent of Birmingham's population were recorded as being from an ethnic minority. By the time of the 2001 census that percentage had risen to 30 per cent, the vast majority of whom were born and bred in the city. This is a growing and young population, representing 40 per cent of the school intake in January 2000. Not surprisingly Birmingham's culture is expressing the cosmopolitan nature of its new population. Fusion is everywhere: in the food, in the films, in the accent, in the music. Birmingham's youth, who are colour blind, glean and plunder from all the cultures they come across and what is created is fresh, new and now is becoming special to Birmingham.

For us at Shillam + Smith the challenge was to tap into that trend – to design for Birmingham's new population in a way that would respond to these fertile cultural fusions we saw going on around us. We had a series of strong values that we wanted to adhere to. These included a wish to stay away from pastiche and not to patronize any section of the community. We also wanted to start to create architecture which everyone in Birmingham, whatever their ethnic origins, would feel some affinity with.

The Splash of Colour Project

Fortunately, part of our consultation work included a modest budget for environmental improvements. The figure was too small to make any real difference to an area of several square miles and a population of 50,000 people. We wanted to use this money to help change the way people felt about their area, to understand what Saltley and Small Heath might become if local energies were harnessed. We also wanted to include those people who are often excluded from a dialogue about regeneration, who do not go to public meetings or feel confident enough to participate. We have a predominantly young population in this area; it is the children who will inherit the results of our decisions today. We also wanted to start a dialogue with more sheltered women, who often do not feel able to participate, and sometimes are not encouraged to do so.

At the same time we happened to be undertaking a study in London, sponsored by the London Arts Board, on how public art could be used in the public consultation process. I felt that in Saltley and Small Heath there existed the ideal territory to commence such a programme. To the astonishment of our steering group and to the bemusement of the local community we set about persuading them of the benefits of the exercise. It is to their credit that after listening to our proposals they gave us the go-ahead and considerable support and encouragement to set up this environmental art project.

Six artists created six different projects, each one temporary and each one related to a specific issue of consultation. The work explored issues relating to housing, a healthy lifestyle, use of public open space, the nature of expectation in regeneration and the identity of the area. All the works were temporary and located within the public domain. In an area of wide ethnic mix the potential to communicate with people outside the confines of cultural stereotypes and using non-verbal methods is vital. Pervaiz Khan, one of the contributing artists, who made a video *Visions – a Portrait of Small Heath* with school kids and projected it onto a huge external screen opposite one of the popular take-aways on Coventry Road, said this:

> Birmingham is a comparatively young city, considering that some of its inhabitants have links to places where there were sophisticated cities four thousand years ago. Yet the future always lies with the youth. If some of the young people who I met at a local school as part of working on 'Visions' are fortunate enough to continue to make art into adulthood, they could play a crucial part in redefining the image of Birmingham, rising out of the ashes of an industrial past.

Housing Outcome

For us the most powerful outcome of this project was the inspiration it gave us in designing new housing for the area. Children working with the artist Nicola Morriss had given us fantasy tales of their dream home. What recurs in their fantasy was the need for space. Many of these children live in large extended family houses and often in cramped conditions. The schism of Midlands Architecture and the Designed Environment (MADE), funded by the Commission for Architecture and the Built Environment (CABE), will deliver.

The 2008 Capital of Culture bid could also encourage good modern architecture through the promotion of an exemplary project which is not a single landmark building but a mixed use neighbourhood with imaginative homes, offices, healthcare buildings and schools. In this respect it would be similar to the Stuttgart Weissenhof exhibition of 1927 or the recent Homes ot the Future development which Glasgow promoted as part of its successful bid as City of Culture 1990.

In summary, Birmingham should not try too hard to impress but learn to enjoy itself and be proud of its culture and skills – in short, make the ordinary extraordinary.

Chapter 5

Acts of Madness
An interview with Will Alsop

Liam Kennedy

Liam Kennedy Do you have early visual memories of Birmingham or the region?

Will Alsop For family reasons I've been visiting the West Midlands for longer than I can remember. I was born and bred in Northampton but had close family links with Walsall. The highlight of trips was going to downtown Birmingham. When it registered consciousness was immediately post Rotunda, Bull Ring, all that, that was brand new architecture, that was a brave new world. I remember Birmingham being the epitome of modernity. I remember people making movies about the wonders of the car being this moving platform from which to view the city. This was the future – in a sense it has been the future, but that bit of the future is worn out now and we need a new one.

LK There are people working at making a new Birmingham. The city is caught up in the drive of many post-industrial cities – to rebrand, to mint a new image.

WA I don't like the term branding very much, but I know what you mean, it's the usual term and it's not a bad thing. I am very happy that Birmingham and West Bromwich want to offer something to the world completely different to other British cities.

LK I want to talk in more detail about what these cities are doing in that respect. First, though, a few questions on your career and outlook. Would it be true to say you were discovered in Europe before Britain? Has your time come?

WA If it has, I'm comfortable enough. I'm 55, taken long enough. Your main ambition is to maintain some integrity in what you struggle to get done.

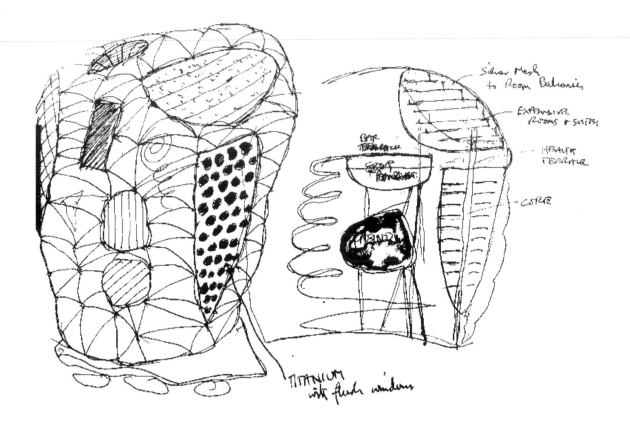

Silver Mesh
to Room Balconies

EXPENSIVE
ROOMS & SUITES

HEALTH
TERRACE

CORE

BAR
TERRACE

TITANIUM
with flush windows

5.1
Concept sketch for mixed-use development at Birmingham Mass House Circus, 2001

In 1984 the telephone rang and it was Hamburg and Hamburg gave me some wonderful opportunities. In the 1980s and 1990s they didn't worry about your architectural pedigree, they worried about what you were saying. Whereas here there was and still is the aversion to risk and therefore you are a risk always and that is how you are assessed. In Hamburg they were prepared to take risks and that has spilled over into work in Holland and other places. I also had an office in Moscow for 10 years. I went to Moscow because that was my risk. I had no illusion I would produce great architecture. I went to experience and be a part of a city undergoing change at a more rapid pace than our cities here.

LK Has something happened within Britain that has made it more receptive to architecture you are interested in, architecture that is not just high tech, 'polite modernism'?

WA I think it was enormously helpful that in the run-up to the election in 1997 there was talk of design and culture being important. New Labour has been disappointing in lots of ways but on the whole has gone in the right direction. That's one strand. Another strand is . . . Gehry did build that extraordinary building in Bilbao. I'm so jealous of that, I think that is fabulous. I like the idea you can build such an icon, an extraordinary spatial experience. Most politicians can't conceive of that and

5.2
New Street Station, Birmingham, 2003

therefore they've never asked for it. If anything, they kill risk, but because of Bilbao they've had to rethink that strategy a bit.

LK In Birmingham as in many other cities there are splits between those saying we need a Bilbao-effect building and those saying that the urge to get one is working against addressing broader socio-economic issues of regeneration.

WA Birmingham has been engaged in such a debate for a long time. I remember going to the Highbury meeting in late 1988. I recall some exciting discussion. For example, if you put in a fast train link to Heathrow, then Heathrow becomes Birmingham Airport – why not? – if we worry about sustainability and celebration then we have to get people there.

LK Speaking of transport, you have been given the job to undertake New Street Station's redesign, but what exactly have you been asked to do?

WA I can cautiously answer that. There is one very pragmatic issue – the first part of the brief is how to make the station safe to use until 2020 as the number of users increases. If you speak to the Strategic Rail Authority (SRA), they're saying there is not much money but, whatever we spend on New Street, we want to be the first step in a much more radical review. Our job is to think of an endgame and think of how the first element fits into that. What interests me about New Street Station is that it is in the centre of a large city. That's quite unique. But the Pallasades – one of the worst multi-storey car parks in the world – what were they thinking? But then it was a brave new world and I can imagine that the Pallasades must have seemed marvellous. How do you give value to the Pallasades? The answer is you build a proper station. That means light, airy, clear, spatial experience.

LK You have said: 'West Bromwich needs an attraction. Not something added vicariously like a theme park, but a place that reflects its belief in itself . . . The key thing is that c/PLEX [The Public Building] will be community driven' (Glancey 2002). (See colour plate 5)

WA The Public project has been a very seminal project from my personal point of view and I've learned a lot from doing it. Eighty per cent of what I now espouse about public consultation came from this project (and 75 per cent of that came from Sylvia King). You might have ideas about access and engagement with people but if you don't know who they are you're fxxxxd. Sylvia and her team knew, and so we could have a whole series of workshops, with the young and the old, cultural minorities and majorities. There was a model I formulated through working with The Public Building that I've gone on to use in Barnsley and Rotterdam and one or two other places. People should be invited

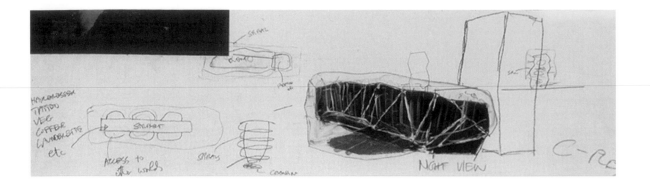

5.3
Detail of Will Alsop drawing for c/PLEX Project, 2001

to be part of a creative engagement, not asked to respond to something – asked to create something. The only rule in sessions is you cannot say anything negative, you must say positive things (not, you'll never get this off the ground; rather, what we need is . . .). Get people to write descriptions, to draw. I take that away and then play it back to them. This does not undermine my sense of myself as an architect; it is a combination between their acts of madness and my own acts of madness.

LK   Drawings, abstraction – how do we get from that to buildings?

WA   There are several different levels of abstraction, different levels of imagination. On one level there is work I do in my garden hut and this feeds your imagination. Work with interest groups and their creativity feeds another level of imagination, moderated by the first one. On The Public Building, for example, we had early general agreement on what kind of building was wanted. Then we went into a period of six weeks, designing a different building each week. Sylvia [King] and David [Patton] came to my Norfolk hut to discuss and out of that process came the circulation, the spiral, which is still there today – you're going in, going up, and working your way down. That was the approach: let's unpick it and see in a short period of time if there is anything else we can discover about this building – and there was – and you go into what I call 'suspended decision-making mode'. If I was writing an instruction manual, I'd say never take a decision until you have to, always keep it open. I'd encourage you to fall in love with every aspect of the process, but you never fall in love forever. (See colour plate 6)

LK   Is that the basis of a design philosophy?

WA   That's too grand a phrase. We are living in a period that has no predominant architectural style, theory, philosophy and I think that's fantastic – it's the first time in architectural history when you could say that. Is there anything we can log onto, to make a start, and then comes in the idea of creativity – the painting and drawing – they're all clues. I've done exercises with students where I've said I want you to design a really ugly building. Of course, they find it much harder, but sometimes it's fantastic, better that what they do if they wear their architect's hat.

LK With the evolution of The Public Building there have been ups and downs with planners and with efforts to secure funding. What has this done to your passion and plans for the building?

WA Planners say all the things they think they're supposed to say. There is nothing creative in what they have to say, just churning out a mantra – scale, colour, etc. Yet, they understand they have got to change. It is a question of whether you engage with change and make something of it and I'm not sure planners in West Bromwich have yet really engaged with that as a thought. On one level, they know that, spatially, West Bromwich is complete crap – as a place it's not a place – and so they're very happy for big companies to walk all over them. They're of that mindset that they're very happy that anyone is going to spend some money in West Bromwich. They don't realize their own power to say no and that through the planning process they can get something better. However, I think we've come a long way in West Bromwich. When I first got the job they wanted to build the building on the edge of town, which wouldn't have had any effect. So we engaged in that debate and succeeded in moving it to the former bus station, so it is in the middle of a public square – it *will* be great. And West Bromwich is in a very fortunate position of having an organization like The Public that can programme that public space.

LK Do you have a sense that the arts are becoming motors for urban regeneration?

WA Well, in one sense artists have long been associated with urban regeneration. We know that story, as with SoHo in New York: artists move in because it's cheap, they change the ambience and then others with more money move in and artists move somewhere else – they act as agents of change. But in the case of West Bromwich it's different. What I found in Jubilee is an organization that has authority and longevity; they have been well backed by the local authority for a long period of time. What they do may even be construed as an important part of the social services budget – people can talk to artists more readily than doctors . . .

LK You have used the phrase 'big architecture' to address relations between planning and architecture. Is The Public Building an example?

WA Yes. 'Big Architecture' refers to the relationship between planning and the experience of walking around it, or looking at it. Most urban design and planning is abstract and I want to make it real. You have to be prepared to draw what it will look like. Internally, in The Public Building there are lots of radical curves and bumps – the simplicity of outside is in contrast with the complexity of inside – we have a struggle to make it even more complex. I have a passion for Piranesi, for the endless space, no edges to the space – I think The Public Building will feel considerably larger than it really is.

Part II

Interventions

Chapter 6

Making Mansions

Sylvia King

When I was a child we lived opposite some waste ground. It was, with the exception of a narrow path that ran through it, overgrown with tall grass and rosebay willowherb. Me and my mates made mansions there. We'd tread the grass into long and intricate corridors, the flowers made way for palatial rooms too numerous to count and complicated sagas were enacted for hours and days on end. The world was very real to us, because the walls seemed so substantial. Only the tallest of us (and that would never be me!) could peer over the grass. This plot was next to a school with a high wall, which at some point fell down. Then for the next few years we also had red bricks to mark out our mansion, we could now make seats and tables and very daringly venture into the woods that belonged to the school. Of course the most important thing about this 'architecture' was that it was the backdrop, the platform on which to enact our dramas (often inspired by such Saturday cinema epics as *Spartacus*, *Ben Hur*, or more alarmingly *The Nun's Story* – no *cinéma vérité* for us, thank you).

My next venture into this strange and yet commonplace world of architecture and buildings was when they were building a new secondary school close by. We'd climb rudimentary stairs and dangerous ladders to the roof, four floors up, and one of the favoured activities was putting your toes over the edge of the building . . . When anyone mentions 'the built environment', I can't help thinking of brick tables and grass corridors and the terror of our small feet over the edge of a four-storey building.

I joined Jubilee Arts (now The Public) in 1979 and realized I was with a group of people who were making their own way, creating meaning in their own back yard. Now I am in my fifteenth year as leader of The Public and we are embarked on a £40 million project to put a real, yet fantastical Will Alsop building – The Public Building – in the middle of West Bromwich, some four or five miles from that piece of waste ground. As a new home for Jubilee Arts, in many ways it will serve the same purpose as those grass corridors: as a platform for a whole range of creative activities. There will be

the space to do our project work with people, as well as learning opportunities, conference and events space, workspace for creative industries and a show case for arts work that questions what art is, who does it and where they do it. It will also provide a chance for the public to participate in that debate and influence the content, in other words a platform to enact dramas; as Will Alsop says, it will be 'a box of delights'. The building will sit in the middle of a new public square, in itself a result of collaboration between Jubilee and Sandwell Metropolitan Borough Council (MBC).

The building involves those same elements of aspiration and risk (grass mansions and experiments on the fourth floor!). Not enough of it around in my view. Maybe we're all frightened to aspire in case we get disappointed, and we've beaten the hell out of that word risk. There are fewer bits of ground to play on and, yes, I know we should never have been able to get into that building site, but it's certain you wouldn't be able to now. Kids get taken to school by car; they play in the street much less. Our public space is more precious than at any time, so what might The Public do to redress the shift, to reclaim some of it? And how did Jubilee Arts dream up such an unlikely scheme?

Making Waves

Jubilee was born in 1974, the same year the Borough of Sandwell, its home, was created (an artificial bit of local government reorganization uniting the towns of West Bromwich, Wednesbury, Rowley Regis, Cradley Heath, Smethwick, Tipton and Oldbury). The project was part of the wider manifestation of 'arts for everyone' that had been inspired by a range of social and political actions in the 1960s and 1970s. The student riots in France, sit-ins and 'actions' at universities and art colleges up and down the country here, the Mexican muralists and their role in revolution, UNESCO's pronouncements on culture and democracy – all had informed an idealistic and demanding post-war generation. Community theatre got there first, taking plays out of the theatre and onto the streets: 7:84, Shared Experience, Monstrous Regiment of Women to name a very few. Joan Littlewood had blazed a trail and others confidently took it forward. Locally, the likes of Charles Parker had already introduced 'actuality' recording to radio in his radio ballads in the 1950s. The arrival of the midget tape recorder had meant that you could record outside the studio and his belief in the poetry of local voices meant that for the first time accents other than those of the establishment were heard on radio. It's taken for granted now but was hugely significant in both technological and cultural terms. In 1974, Parker set up Banner Theatre in the West Midlands, a campaigning and political theatre group who are still around.

Throughout the 1970s and 1980s experimentation went wild – community publishing, print shops, bookshops and darkrooms all began to flourish. In London the creation of the first Arts Lab spawned others around the country, including one in Birmingham. These were independent, non-establishment, very experimental arts venues that brought together a range of disciplines (or lack of them!) from cinema and photography to theatre. All of the touring groups above were seen at Birmingham Arts Lab in the theatre while *The Discreet Charm of the Bourgeoisie* was shown with (those very scary things) subtitles in the cinema. By the 1980s Derek Bishton and others were producing that legendary photography magazine *10:8* in rooms upstairs and the Birmingham Film and Video Workshop with Roger Shannon and Johnny Turpie was now located there with a local slant on both content and involvement. Molly Randle and John England had set up The Midlands Arts Centre in the grounds of Canon Hill Park in the 1960s and the involvement of people in art-making there was blooming. The location itself was a radical notion, the idea of bringing the arts to a wider public was very new and the establishment was still wary of such hippy ideas.

The wider region was also very lively with radical architect Cedric Price (Will Alsop trained with him) up in the Potteries advocating radical master plans to transform the whole area to what would now be called a cultural quarter: to regenerate, in fact, through cultural activities. Theatre in Education was thriving in Coventry and there were a number of community arts groups establishing themselves: Telford Community Arts, Saltley Print and Action Media, Trinity Arts, Pentabus and of course Jubilee. There were links to others around the country, such as the Blackie in Liverpool, Freeform in London, and Community Arts Work Shop in Manchester. I was on the Board of the Shelton Trust, the national community arts body with its radical mag *Another Standard*. Geoff Simms and Dorothy Wilson were at West Midlands Arts and, all in all, the knock-on effect for the West Midlands region was that there was good debate, lots of rows, but a lot of cross-fertilization of ideas – plenty of chance to challenge received wisdom!

Jubilee itself began as a community theatre enterprise, working in schools and making pub and street theatre. It expanded its base to include video makers, artists (though, at that time, that was proscribed – 'cultural activists' were more favoured) working in print and photography and we bought a bus. That was my first job at Jubilee. The local rag billed it as 'petite brunette swings ten ton double-decker round the streets of Sandwell'. The feminist movement hadn't quite penetrated as far as the Black Country. Still, Kate (the first bus worker) and I revelled in the glory of 'swinging' that bus and the glorious moments when someone would ask for the driver and we'd smile winningly and own that title and watch the jaws drop . . . Oh, what waves we thought we were making.

In fact we *were* making waves or ripples of some kind, locally at least. Sandwell has a population of nearly 300,000. That's the same size as Bradford or Belfast. It has a very small Victorian municipal art gallery/museum in Wednesbury, a 100-seater tiny amateur theatre, and no bookshop (apart from a section in WH Smith and one or two dealing in second-hand books). There's one two-screen cinema (about to close) and an old single screen showing exclusively Asian films. It's hard to imagine that that's all there might be in, say, Belfast! Back in the 1950s and 1960s there were certainly a lot more cinemas (hence my intimate knowledge of the screenplay of *Spartacus*), and dance halls (the Beatles played at the Plaza in Old Hill), but certainly no community centres and the like. Working Men's clubs existed but they belonged to an older tradition and were more like private pubs. Community centres seem, now, to have always been there, but they are relatively recent phenomena. So in the 1970s and early 1980s the Jubilee

6.2
Jubilee's double-decker bus, complete with darkroom, print shop and meeting rooms, 1980

Bus served that purpose – it was a mobile building. Tenants, campaigning about damp or rent rises, met there and made leaflets and posters. Mums met there and made readers for their kids, kids took pictures and developed them in the darkroom on board. Importantly it was about the 'skills and resources to make voices heard' (from Jubilee's mission at the time). The bus was a huge signal; it would arrive where people were and set up shop instantly. Amazingly, I was back on intimate terms with pieces of waste ground, in various locales around the Borough – The Pig and Whistle, The Lost City, The Tump, The Scheme . . . We'd often, particularly on play schemes, transform the space with withies, lanterns, lights, junk sculptures and giant shadow puppet screens to provide a beacon, a destination and improve the whole visual effect of these forgotten yet vital spaces for play and meeting.

So both the bus and the tiny reading room of the old library (our admin base provided by the local authority) served as a platform for a host of activities. The intervention was not just in transforming space but also in changing minds. It was a campaigning time and everybody was against everything – rent rises, the cuts, racism and fascism – and what was needed were spaces to meet and help with how to get heard. People had to help out, learn how to do things, be clear about what they wanted; we couldn't and wouldn't do it all. We made many a video that was used in evidence for a Section 11 (that enabled tenants to take the Council to court if they had problems), a position of opposition. Earlier this year (2002) in a position of partnership, where creative ideas were valued and alternative solutions encouraged, we completed a project on the Lyng estate in West Bromwich. Already the community were on the board of the association that would rede-velop their estate, receiving training and independent advice to be a full part of the decision-making process. The housing workers themselves were enabling, developing a range of relationships. Twenty years earlier this kind of participation and self-help would have been considered subversive. A shift has occurred.

What was our aspiration? Mine was pretty simple: things weren't fair, things weren't equal and that couldn't be right. So locally we needed to get things shifting and changing and globally needed to affect changes in cul-tural policy, so that those changes would last. The word democracy was a very big word for my generation, highly influenced by what was happening politically in America and the effects of the Cold War era. We were saying if we are looking for political and economic democracy, then we must also create the third corner of the triangle: cultural democracy. The UN Declaration of Human Rights states that 'everyone has the right to participate freely in the cultural life of the community'. So the 1970s and 1980s saw big debates about whether there was an equality of access to culture and the arts. It was a fast-moving time. You had the Arts Council of Great Britain, keen to keep up with the times, producing 'The Glory of the Garden' policy to demands for more equity, with Roy Shaw, the Secretary General declaring there would be

'few, but roses' and on the other hand we as cultural activists were responding 'let a thousand flowers bloom'. We were all very big on horticulture around this time . . . a kind of 'growbags for change' theme.

But the issues that were discussed (alongside 'is cinema a legitimate art form?' in the 'Big Arts World') in our sector (the not-very-important community-one) were ones about ownership and agenda setting. We were tapping into the democratic agenda rather than the arts one. These agendas were to last and to inform more than just the arts world. We wanted to change cultural policy; we felt 'the arts' was too narrow a definition. Empowerment, partnership, pluralism and ownership (though the words have now become pieces of jargon) inform most agencies' thinking from housing to health, from learning to regeneration. Again, regeneration departments didn't exist. Yet this is the very work we were engaged in – involving people in the decision-making about their own lives, their own homes, and their own public spaces. We were part of what helped make that shift. Interestingly, Sandwell council now has a department of Urban Form encompassing housing, planning, and highways. It's not that we invented all of this but that we were part of a radical movement in British culture and we aspired to change the world: in fact, many of us dared to try. It became clear that something was going on: the work we engaged in with groups was a form of protest (whether it was publicity about a cause, or an issue-based project) and the amazing result was that in the process of creating the product, the individuals themselves were transformed. They stretched and grew, gained knowledge and confidence and this affected those around them. We had discovered a shared agenda with the Council and other agencies – one of developing the communities' confidence and ability to communicate ideas. Hand in hand with a quality product, this is what creates the change – taking a risk and aspiring to more.

Making Space

By the mid-1980s Jubilee had moved out of the library into a great building Sandwell MBC had refurbished for us and the business was growing. Though our main body of work was Sandwell and the region, we'd worked internationally doing residencies in Poland, Finland and the US and conferences and workshops elsewhere. The demand was growing, there was lots of work to be done and we began to expand to do it. We developed some strong links with health and education agencies and won a few awards (including the first interactive BAFTA award for learning). We also began to make big long-term plans and the idea of 'The Big Dream', which subsequently became The Public project, was born. We knew no one was going to start shovelling in loads of revenue money for development, so the Dream was to grow the business but find a way of raising the capital to house it. Surprisingly, this was before the Lottery millions had come on-stream but we talked to many

6.3
Sandwell Committee Against the Cuts, a silkscreen poster produced by Jubilee Arts, 1983

public agencies that might support us with the concept. Most said: lovely idea . . . but it's too big, too hard, too everything. Too risky, was my guess.

Finally, though, someone was brave. We got our first grant for development in 1994 from the Sandwell Regeneration Partnership. This was to do a feasibility study on the wacky idea I'd somehow sold to the Chief Executive of Sandwell, Nigel Summers, and subsequently to the partnership (the health authority, Business Link, the Training and Enterprise Council and others). It was for £80,000 to develop the idea and put a bid in to the National Lottery, which had come on-stream by then. Nigel was a brave man who had aspirations for the Borough. He'd seen the Borough and particularly the town of West Bromwich lose its edge, lose business and go rapidly into decline. The final straw was Marks and Spencer moving out, it seemed to signal a loss of faith, a statement that said 'people here are poor, they don't want your goods'. It became a loss of confidence, not just for other retailers but also for the inhabitants, the range of agencies that served the public. The knowledge that something big and brave was needed to turn round the fortunes of West Bromwich was easily understood, but the idea that the big brave notion could be a 'community arts centre' was not so easy to sell. We had our prescribed place; we were supposed to ask for a new minibus and gratefully move on.

The Arts Council, however, backed it with a first grant in 1995 and in 2002 its final award of £17.9 million made it one of the big Capital 1 projects. They were brave too. The final project costs are around £40 million; we've spent around £6 million to date. The funding packages are many and complex. There is money from Europe, from the regional Development Agency (who weren't invented when we began), from New Deal for Communities, a central government initiative, from a finance leasing agreement, from trusts and sponsors. But most importantly a total of around £6 million from Sandwell Council, including the land but excluding staff support they loaned us frequently and the cash flow and short-term loans they continue to provide to service this complex funding pie.

This is, to me, one of the most significant developments of all. After all, there we were, funded by the Council, frequently proving a thorn in their side, yet we sought dialogue constantly, we'd listen and respond to many points of view and we had the confidence of those we worked with both in the community and the council. The respect that develops after 27 years of being true to what you believe. What's more, we had a good idea. Our notion was simply to pull the pieces together in a beautiful space: the work we do with communities and with learning opportunities; add to that a chance to set up a new business; include the space for debate, clubbing and music or theatre events to revive the town at night; and finally a showcase, a shopfront for the whole enterprise, Gallery X. This interactive gallery takes the topics from the project work and brings together the public, artists, designers, and videomakers and entwines them as part of the 'national conversation' (Matarasso 1997).

6.4
Members of Jubilee Arts explore the site for The Public Building, the old West Bromwich bus station, 2002

So Sandwell MBC will help us tread the grass down to create the corridors. They've already made the ring road two-way. They'll help us with the bricks to create the palace, (though actually there's not a brick in sight, it's steel and rose-coloured glass). And they and the other funding partners are prepared to put their toes over the edge of a great height to make it possible. Sandwell have embraced the idea as the catalyst for regeneration and been prepared to back a small voluntary group to achieve something huge, whilst being one of the poorest boroughs in the country, with massive challenges facing it from health to housing to high unemployment. But that's why we've done it; we've been in the borough a long time and seen a range of needs. It was evident that we couldn't just do more work but had to contribute to some big changes, changes in policy and changes in aspiration – most importantly, to change the idea that 'nothing good ever happens around here', that 'poor people' don't need or want quality. It's vital that quality buildings and public space are created, particularly for challenged communities, to return a sense of dignity and of hope and the acknowledgement that it is deserved. The cycle needs to be broken. The fabric of the town needs to be rewoven to break that cycle and realize the buried potential of a vibrant community. The Public Building and the public square can then be the platform to enact the stories, the dramas of that community on a remade piece of waste ground.

Chapter 7

Public Art, Civic Identity and the New Birmingham

Tim Hall

Introduction: Summer, 1991

The headlines in the local press at the time spelt it out: 'Proud day for nation's most progressive city' (Hastilow 1991), 'Royal visitors set the seal on city's rebirth' (*Birmingham Post* 1991), 'A symphony of new life for the city' (Morley 1991) and 'Jewel in our crown' (*Evening Mail* 1991). The summer of 1991 was a significant time in the history of Birmingham. The opening, by the Queen, of the International Convention Centre (ICC) in June 1991 was heralded within the city as the culmination of eight years of hard work by the City Council and other influential figures to turn the city's fortunes around. The event was almost universally heralded within Birmingham as marking the birth of a new Birmingham, a transformation from a prosaic, provincial, industrial city to a vibrant, cultured, futuristic, international metropolis. Although the primary motivation behind the development of the ICC was economic, the moment of the ICC's opening was felt as something cultural, almost emotional, a change in the 'idea' of Birmingham, its identity and its image. Birmingham felt like a confident city, a city on the up. It is probably fair to say that all of the considerable transformations of Birmingham's central landscape since 1991 have been predicated on the seismic shift in the idea of Birmingham that occurred around 1991 as the new Birmingham began to emerge.

Moments of civic transformation such as this tend to get portrayed in overly simplistic terms as seamless and unproblematic. The reality is much more messy – such transformations are complex, incomplete and require negotiation as they are inevitably contested moments. The process is far more complex than one set of, in this case post-industrial, identities being inserted in place of another set of, in this case industrial, identities. Despite appearances to the contrary, cities do not completely change overnight. Rather, elements of the old city linger within the new, sometimes as relics, but often deliberately written into the landscapes and identity of the new city. I want to use this as a starting point to highlight some of the complexities of the transformation of Birmingham and the ways in which elements of its past were important to the imagination of a new Birmingham. Specifically I want to look at the role of public art and ask: what role can public art play in the negotiation, reproduction and transformation of civic identity? In doing so I want to consider one important yet problematic aspect of the civic identity of Birmingham: industry. This is explored primarily through a reading of Raymond Mason's statue *Forward*.

Regeneration and the New Birmingham

The extensive regeneration of Birmingham's central area from the mid-1980s onwards was an ambitious attempt to capture inward investment and rejuvenate the city's built environment, its externally perceived image and its battered civic pride (Hubbard 1996; Loftman and Nevin 1998). These efforts were centred around the redevelopment of the Broad Street area, a corridor stretching out of the city centre to the west. The area was intended as a major business tourist attraction. The anchor to this development was the £180 million American-style ICC (with a Hyatt Hotel attached). Other developments included the National Indoor Arena, the rejuvenation of the Gas Street canal basin for leisure use and the complete redesign of Centenary Square, adjacent to the ICC. As part of this process a number of new public artworks were commissioned to be placed within prominent civic spaces, especially those in and around the ICC. Birmingham City Council's investment in public art in the late 1980s was one of the heaviest by a local authority in the UK at the time and demonstrated the extent to which public art had become central to the regeneration of British cities by the 1990s. Although initially promoted from outside the authority by local arts advocates, the idea of incorporating public art into the city's new urban spaces was enthusiastically embraced by the authority (Sargent 1996).

Public art commissioned in association with the ICC included the redesign and paving of Centenary Square by the artist Tess Jarey, who worked alongside the city's landscape design team on all aspects of the square's design. In addition to this, four new pieces of public art were commissioned for Centenary Square along with four for the ICC and one adjacent to its canalside entrance. The most prominent new piece of public art in the city was Raymond Mason's fibreglass statue *Forward*. Costing £275,000, *Forward* was the largest single commission by a provincial UK city for a work of public art at the time of its unveiling in 1991 (Weideger 1991: 14). The statue was located in Centenary Square facing the ICC and narrates a mythical history of Birmingham, giving particular prominence to the city's industrial past. References to industry also occur in two other artworks in the square, David Patten's *Monument to John Baskerville – Industry and Genius*, and Tom Lomax's fountain *Spirit of Enterprise*. In addition to these new sculptures, industry has long been an important subject for civic statuary in Birmingham city centre. With the addition of the four new sculptures, by 1991 there were 14 open-air sculptures in the area around the ICC. Of these, ten were either devoted exclusively to industrial subjects or contained significant industrial references.

Incongruous Industry

The landscapes of the new Birmingham are situated within two sharply contrasting contexts. On the one hand, they fit into the international landscapes of post-industrial, postmodern urbanism, landscapes of convention centres, waterside developments, futuristic architecture and upscale urban consumption. However, on the other, they are everyday landscapes through which Birmingham's citizens live their lives and which provide cultural resources from which senses of the city's identity are drawn. Public art, in being a prominent aspect of both the landscapes of urban regeneration (featured regularly in the local, national and international media, for example) and explicit explorations of civic identity and history, is caught particularly sharply between these two contexts. Advocates of public art claim it is able to make a number of contributions to the regeneration of urban areas (Miles 1997; Hall and Robertson 2001). Public art, in prominent city centre settings, certainly has an important role to play in 'selling' cities to a range of external audiences (Goodey 1994; Hall 1995). However, advocates also argue it can make significant contributions to local cultural identities. Vivian Lovell, then director of the Public Art Commissions Agency in Birmingham, outlined her

7.1
***Forward*, by Raymond Mason, 1991**

vision for a public art programme for the city, 'to develop a public art programme that is unique to Birmingham, reflecting its history, resources, industries, international links and multicultural heritage' (Lovell 1988). Of the programme, Graham Shaylor, then director of development at the City Council, later said: 'The City of Birmingham firmly believes that artworks contribute to the environment and unify a city, bringing together a populace' (Shaylor 1989: 73). These two contexts then, the international and the local, demand careful negotiation if new urban landscapes are to appeal to both international and local audiences.

Initially, the presence of so many references to industry, and especially the stark, working-class industrial iconography of *Forward*, within the city centre's new public art programme seems incongruous. Why would a city seeking to position itself on the international stage and in so doing seek to rid itself of its associations with industry and with the past, saturate its most prominent post-industrial, postmodern, new landscapes with so many references to this very past? The answer lies in the city's need not to lose sight of the local while aspiring to the global, and in the selectivity of the aspects of the industrial past that are incorporated into the city's new landscapes.

Problematic Industry

Economic history often forms an important component of regional identity (Eyles and Peace 1990); this has certainly been true of Birmingham and the Midlands. Nationally, however, industrial identities have long since been viewed in a negative light. A number of writers have recognized what they refer to as 'a rhetorical critique of industrialism' as an enduring characteristic of English culture (Fussell 1980: 151; Wiener 1981; Chambers 1991). In the context of post-industrial urban regeneration, industry is even more problematic as an identity for a city or region to possess and is in sharp contrast to those images that most commentators now deem desirable (Kearns and Philo 1993; Short *et al.* 1993; Gold and Ward 1994; Hall 2001). A history of industry then is both a problematic and contested terrain from which to imagine new civic identities through projects of urban regeneration.

Equally, there were significant local and national anxieties about British industry during the 1980s, as the industrial base of the country contracted in the face of international competition, that added more recent, and arguably more pressing, layers to the negatively held views of industry within the country. First was the apparent low productivity and low quality of British labour, particularly in the face of new working practices, technology and labour organization in the rapidly growing economies of the Far East. The commonly held failings of British industry included poor management, archaic working practices, a lack of innovation and underinvestment. Second, there were considerable anxieties expressed through the media and political

7.2
Spirit of Enterprise fountain,
Centenary Square, Birmingham, 2003

discourse about both the disruptive potential of organized, unionized labour and the union as an impediment to industrial modernization.

During this time these failings were regarded as deeply embedded within the industrial cultures of the industrial heartlands of the UK, especially the Midlands. In addition to the severe deindustrialization of the region, by the early 1980s Birmingham had gained a reputation for the production of shoddy products by a highly unionized, militant labour force. Its reputation derived in large part from the troubled course of the British Leyland car factory in Longbridge, in the south Birmingham suburbs. The company became synonymous with the production of unreliable, outdated 'Friday' cars and during 1978 and 1979 was involved in industrial disputes and financial and management crises that received extensive coverage in the national media. A BBC television documentary summed up the image of the city of Birmingham during this period:

> The international image of Birmingham was, for years, determined by the events at British Leyland. The impression was of a city wedded to a disruptive and powerful workforce, constantly at odds with a weak management. Despite a government rescue, the company was in crisis, and to outsiders, so was the city. Increasingly it gained a reputation for outdated industries and shoddy products. (BBC2 1991)

The reconstruction of Birmingham's image in the 1990s was thus caught between two competing imperatives. On the one hand was the historical importance of industry to the identity of the city and region; on the other was a series of negative associations that had become attached to the idea of industry by the 1980s.

Meanings of Industry

'Industry' has not had a single fixed, fast meaning throughout history. Rather, its meaning changed in the years around 1800 (Williams 1958; 1976). The shifts in meanings of words, such as industry, reflect wider transformations in the economy and culture. Words are capable of acquiring new meanings and these meanings are open to selective and partial recovery and representation. In the case of industry, which is so closely associated with the identity of certain places, this suggests that spatial identities are also not stable and immutable but open to alternative meanings and transformation through representation and reuse. The selective recovery of the meanings of certain keywords strongly associated with place, civic or regional identity, may be a tactic employed in the re-imagination of these spatial identities.

Prior to the emergence of industrial capital in the late eighteenth century, 'industry' referred to a human attribute 'which could be paraphrased as "skill, assiduity, perseverance, diligence"' (Williams 1958: 13–19). It is a meaning still present in the adjective 'industrious'. It was only later after the mass industrialization of the British economy that 'industry' came to refer to 'manufacturing and productive institutions, and . . . their general activities' (Williams 1958: 13). While the original meaning of industry evoked the 'higher' realms of human endeavour, skill and achievement, its subsequent meaning is more associated with the 'baser', and currently unfashionable, activities of production. In the context of the representation of industry in programmes of urban regeneration, this presents both problems and possibilities. On the one hand, it suggests the possibility of positive images of industry derived from its original meaning; on the other, however, are the problems attached to its subsequent meaning. In the (re)presentation of industry to contemporary audiences, in the context of urban regeneration, it is apparent that some semantic fixing and selectivity are required to ensure that the desired meanings prevail.

Industry, Public Art and Urban Regeneration

Representations of industry dominate the ICC's public art programme. Of the four new pieces of public art in Centenary Square, three were exclusively concerned with industrial subjects or made some references to them. The most prominent element of the ICC's public art programme is Raymond Mason's fibreglass sculpture *Forward*. *Forward* explores the emergence of Birmingham's civic identity through the figurative representation of a number of 'Brummies', and is replete with references to various historical periods. The narrative is dynamic and temporal, growing in size from a smoke-filled Victorian scene to the present day. Two issues emerge from a reading of the presence of industry in this statue. First is the reaffirmation of the centrality of industry to the identity of the city. Second is the artist's assertion of Birmingham's industrial history as a human, rather than a mechanical story.

Industry occupies a space within the sculpture between a grim, urban past and a bright future symbolized by the ICC. The significance of this space is that it is here, Mason argues, that a recognizable civic identity emerged. Human figures increase in both size and detail to become distinguishable as individuals rather than merely members of a crowd. References to specific individuals, activities and institutions begin to appear at this point.

The representation of industry in *Forward* does not seek either to exclude the functional elements of industry or to make reference to industry solely through recognizable pioneers or industrial heroes. Rather, the story of industry in the statue is one of ordinary working men, incidentally largely ignoring the role of women in Birmingham's industrial history, engaged in a process of production. However, Mason reconciles industry's unappealing functionality through a very humanized reading of the process. This he achieves through mythologizing Birmingham's industry as a human rather than mechanical saga:

> 'For one precise moment in history Birmingham was unique,' says
> Mason . . . 'It founded a tradition of fine craftsmanship and fine
> machinery. That shouldn't be forgotten.' Nor will it if Mason
> achieves his aim . . . 'They tore the heart out of Birmingham . . .
> It would be a great pity to forget what was a great moment in the
> human saga of fine work.'
>
> (Weideger 1991: 14)

Mason's regard for Birmingham's industrial history lying in its human rather
than mechanical elements is clear in *Forward*. The representation of the
human and mechanical elements are not to scale and are biased towards
the human. (See colour plate 7) The human figures are also heavily idealized.
Rather than focusing on specific, recognizable individuals, the figures in the
industrial scene are constructed as archetypes of particular human attributes,
most obviously skill and strength. There is a strong echo, too, in these figures
of the city's coat of arms, which also venerates the contribution of industry
to the city through the presence of an idealized figure of an industrial
workman. This mythology posits the origins of Birmingham's identity in the
body rather than the machine.

The public artworks commissioned as part of the recent regeneration of the centre of Birmingham clearly represent an attempt to
commemorate a prominent aspect of civic pride within Birmingham and its
region. However, they also seek to provide specific correctives to the negative, contested and unstable meanings attached to industry during the 1980s.
They are examples of the selective recovery of industry's meanings. The
most prominent themes of these representations are that they represent
industry as a skilled, and as an essentially human, individual, process. In
doing so they act as powerful correctives to those anxieties about the disruptive potential of organized labour and the perceived low quality of the British
worker. At a time of severe deindustrialization in the UK economy *Forward*
reasserts the integrity of Birmingham and British labour, while achieving a
delicate balancing act between local mythologies of industrial pride and
national political discourses of industrial reorganization. In retelling stories of
the city's history and identity it connects with local cultural identities and in
presenting industry as a 'human saga' (Raymond Mason, in Weideger 1991:
14), it sanitizes a potentially unappealing image, negotiating a potentially
disruptive insertion into the landscapes of a new, remade Birmingham.

Conclusion

This chapter has sought to demonstrate that remaking Birmingham has
involved the incorporation of elements of the old into the new city. The
'remade' Birmingham is situated in two sharply contrasting contexts – the
international context of post-industrial, postmodern cities, eager to influence

and attract global flows of capital, and the local context of lived in, everyday spaces and places. In recognizing this, Birmingham sought not to lose sight of the local as it strived to become international.

Public art is a medium caught particularly acutely between these two potentially competing contexts, given its contributions to both selling cities to external audiences and rejuvenating public cultures and senses of local and civic identity. In weaving elements of local cultural identity and tradition into the new Birmingham it is clear that some degree of selectivity and manipulation was required. This is not to say that the myths of industry present in *Forward* and other pieces of public art in Birmingham city centre are not true, merely that they represent only one amongst a number of truths.

Finally, discussions about the remaking of cities in a postmodern era have tended to be dominated by the voices of writers, critics and academics keen to demonstrate their ability to deconstruct the ideological and symbolic meanings of new urban landscapes. To date, too little attention has been paid to the voices of ordinary citizens whose cities have been reshaped, who live with these landscapes every day and whose experiences would validate or refute the theses put forward by others. Too little attention has been paid to ordinary, everyday experiences of remade cities and the meanings their publics derive from them. Perhaps it is time for this silence to be addressed.

Chapter 8

Off-site

Deborah Kermode

The Ikon Gallery operates a diverse programme of projects and exhibitions that vary in scale, duration, development time and location, involving artists from the UK and abroad. Occurring within a context of assertive urban regeneration, the off-site programme focuses largely on actual human experience. By challenging existing frameworks for artists, each project occupies a new site, working alongside a potentially new audience. The off-site programme brings together a unique series of projects that, at their heart, propose a more generous approach to artistic practice and are characterized by their location away from the gallery. They articulate a desire to make an art that has continuity with the physical environment, transcending the often formulaic restraints of a gallery situation, engaging with a public who may have little or no experience of art and with public spaces in which art is absolutely not the priority.

Emphasis is therefore placed on audience participation, asserting not only a democracy of familiar and ordinary objects, often through the use of the ready-made, but also a recognition and collaborative interdependence between artists and non-artists. There is a stress on process rather than product, with significance placed on the 'doing' and taking part, as much as the finished product, should there be one. The methodology behind the production of much off-site work, its temporality and unforced fluidity place it in contrast with established perceptions of public art as frequently anachronistic or irrelevant to the very public it was ostensibly created 'for'. In the past, works of art have often been created somewhat separately from the material world they inhabit and this continues into the presentation and consequent reception of the work. Ikon commissions off-site work in a much more active mode, with a realization that the process is a valuable and often integral part of the work.

The off-site programme sits well alongside the current urban renaissance in Birmingham, which embraces a wide range of cultural possibilities and amplifies the city's diversity of cultural practice with temporary (often site-specific) work, passing activities and performative events. Ikon is fundamentally a creature of Birmingham's reinvention – born in the 1960s' Bull Ring and developing into an organization that has moved position, both geographically and culturally, to the meeting point of the many communities of the city. There exists a synchronicity between the off-site programme and the ever-changing nature of the city and its inhabitants, who perhaps are used to witnessing and 'taking part' in this constant reinvention. Influenced by the richness and diversity of the communities and the visual composition of Birmingham, many artists have made work that investigates the character and spirit of the city, at a time when the demographics and the landscape are under rapid change. Much of the programme results from the artists' investigations of Birmingham that are often long-term and derived from less obvious features of the city.

As part of the group exhibition, *Birmingham* (Ikon 2001), Swiss artist Beat Streuli created an off-site element to his work in which he photographed a selection of the young people he met whilst visiting secondary schools in the city. Rather than depict a portrait of a physical city, Streuli chose to represent the young people that energize it. The exhibition title itself is uncompromising and unapologetic, challenging the tiresome and outdated notion of the city as being somewhat unfashionable. Presented as a 27 metre billboard and located in the heart of the city centre, this series

8.1
Ikon Gallery, 2003

8.2
Beat Streuli, *Birmingham Portraits,*
2001. Photo Gary Kirkham

of seven portraits elevated the young people to iconic status and signified the extraordinary cultural diversity of Birmingham.

In a similar vein, Navin Rawanchaikul's project, *Shakespeare in Taxi,* began with hours of informal conversations between the artist and taxi drivers about their experiences of working in Birmingham. Rawanchaikul focused on the reminiscences of taxi drivers, recognizing that in this city of immigration, many of the drivers come from a diversity of cultural backgrounds. Their day-to-day experiences take them back and forth across the city, each time collecting a new fare that inevitably leads to a new conversation. These stories formed the raw material for a comic book distributed freely from the backseats of city taxis. Like the large photographic billboard images by Streuli, with their familiar, corporate genre of advertising, here Rawanchaikul also transferred his ideas into an accessible and practical format – a comic – thus allowing the public to own a part of this artistic intervention.

During 2000 Ikon organized a large, group exhibition under the title of *As It Is* (Ikon 2000), the premise of which was to invite artists to reflect on the character of Birmingham. A number of artists chose to consider the impending demolition of the infamous Bull Ring market area, which had for so long characterized so emphatically the image of Birmingham. Pierre Huyghe's performance video/installation, *Concrete Requiem*, sought to reflect on the current redevelopment and the way in which cities readjust their visionary concerns. When originally unveiled in 1964, the Bull Ring was heralded as the 'most advanced shopping centre in the world' (Cowan 2000). Within two decades it had become a symbol of a city in decline. Huyghe's video celebrates the hard modernist image of what is now perceived as an outdated Birmingham. The video synchronizes the documentation of the city taken by the artist with a composition for a small orchestra derived from the recorded sound. At one point in the video, Huyghe's camera pans to a man sitting at the side of the road watching the traffic pass by, as the sound of continuous gear changes are played by the strings, his small movements absorbed into a context of accelerated urban flux.

In contrast and working more anonymously Margaret Barron uses the medium of traditional oil paint, with its associations of permanence and sentimentality, to create temporary interventions that questioned both subject matter and position. As part of *As It Is*, Barron located her miniature paintings of everyday life (often only a few centimetres in size), on street furnishings such as bus stops, hoardings and lamp-posts, particularly those surrounding the Bull Ring market. These often-mundane necessities of urban life were reinvigorated as unique and profound situations. Moreover, these paintings offered a pertinent reminder that the scenes in question were waiting to be demolished and replaced by a new landscape. Here, the commonplace was pinpointed to act as a testimonial mapping of something lost. The paintings appeared anonymously without signage or signature and though advertised within Ikon's publicity, they appealed to an incidental audience, one that came across the work serendipitously and without intent. Barron, like many artists, deliberately avoids signposting her work, with the hope that it will be seen by a wider public who bring to it a different set of values and experiences than an art constituency.

Many artists have situated their work within the same space as the city's physical changes, thus the public are able to witness the inspiration operating alongside the completed work. The art becomes inherent to the fabric of the city whilst possessing a critical edge, and as such, both share a common purpose and, ultimately, a similar fate. The potential for transformation and interactivity between art and the public is given legitimacy.

Ikon's projects are by their very nature temporary interventions with some of the work destined to be destroyed or disassembled, as in the case of Tadashi Kawamata's jerry-built *Canal Boat* installation or Katharina Grosse's large-scale mural. Equally, uncontrollable external forces can also come into play – theft or adverse weather conditions as with the miniature paintings of Margaret Barron. The work belies non-preciousness and an assertive generosity, as there is no intention to commodify or preserve the work.

This is particularly relevant in the work of Katharina Grosse, whose large-scale painting dominated the façade of Birmingham Central Library, during the autumn of 2002. Stretching over 5 metres high and 30 metres in length to cover glass, concrete and metal, the painting revealed the architectural elements of this imposing 1960s', municipal building. Making a strong impression on the pedestrian experience of Chamberlain Square, the painting produced an intensity of experience, one that moves from inside the frame on the gallery wall to the architectural fabric of a building. Birmingham Central Library became a vast canvas to be covered with this luminous field of strongly coloured spray paint, of which there were over twenty colours including iridescent copper, cobalt teal, burnt umber and fluorescent orange. (See colour plate 8) Situated directly opposite the Birmingham Museum and Art Gallery, with its superb collection of nineteenth-century and modernist paintings, it created an extraordinary dialogue. But unlike these traditionally painted canvases, Grosse's work was of a transitory nature and was seen by many more people who were not intending to have an art experience. When the colour in Katharina Grosse's installations spread freely across the concrete walls and glass windows, to compete with the architecture, it was as though some intrinsically anarchic power of street graffiti also came into play.

There existed an exploration of the space, as if the artist was marking out a territory – most commonly demonstrated by graffiti artists, who perform their own covert artistic interventions on public buildings. However, this spray painting came with a sense of privilege and approved authority. As the artist has said:

> Graffiti makers go to extraordinary lengths to make enormous pieces – maybe very high up – and we don't know who they are. They conceal their identity while they make a big contribution to public life. I don't know if graffiti is an art form. That doesn't matter to me. What matters is that graffiti communicates very strongly and publicly something about the power of people. Graffiti makers also are responding to something, which is already there, to the spaces and to the surfaces as well.

(Grosse 2002: 32)

Though Grosse makes connections with a street aesthetic, her work is concerned with a range of issues that have as much to do with art history as with space and time.

Separated yet inclusive of the real world, Grosse and her volunteers worked behind the screened polythene on the scaffolding, aware of the hustle and bustle of the moving city beyond. On site, the productive labour with all its paraphernalia – safety equipment, generators and fencing – could have been mistaken for building maintenance, until it was of course made fully public. There existed, therefore, a non-hierarchic situation because people could encounter the work as part of their daily routine, it appeared and later disappeared to act as a communal experience. The acquiescent nature of much of the off-site work creates a sense of continuity with the constantly changing city, pertinent in the case of Birmingham Central Library, which is fated for demolition in the near future.

Often, a project is defined site-specifically and the place itself becomes an entity, one in which the viewer's path becomes evident through the exploration of the space. Many of the locations contain free-standing environments that are positioned in context. Tadashi Kawamata chose to focus his project, *Canal Boat*, on the waterways at Brindleyplace, an area that has been vastly regenerated to attract tourism and commercial activity. That *Canal Boat*, a temporary installation converted from the hull of a 21-metre ex-commercial narrowboat, should be made in an area dominated largely by imposing modern architectural styles counterbalances the formal clarity of Kawamata's space, which offered a safe haven from the busy outside world. The project involved a team of volunteers who collaborated with the artist to create a collective spirit, encouraging them to assert their own talents. Passers-by were able to witness the development of the project throughout its two-week installation, making the intention of the project explicit. Its position outdoors represented continuity between the installation and the street, as people were able to stop and watch. On its completion the volunteers occupied the work, this continuity enabled them to share their experiences with visitors in the knowledge that their participation played an invaluable contribution. Therefore there was no definable definition as to where the work began or ended, and this is true of a large proportion of off-site projects that take place in and are part of the material world.

In contrast to Kawamata's externally sited project, American artist, Andrea Zittel explored the notion of temporary environments by inhabiting a derelict warehouse in central Birmingham to create a 'show room', filling the spaces with *A-Z Compartment Units*. These quasi-architectural modules – designed as flat-pack structures made from plywood and glass – became the artist's home for several weeks, stacked next to and on top of each other in different configurations, customized to meet her day-to-day needs. After her departure the installation was open to the public to function as a regular exhibition. Whilst Kawamata worked with his team publicly, Zittel and her group worked semi-privately, with the public able to view the

8.3
Tadashi Kawamata, *Canal Boat*, 2000.
Photo Gary Kirkham

process on the Internet on a daily web page with the real interaction delayed until the experiment had been tested and proved by the artist.

Zittel chose to site *A-Z Compartment Units* inside a derelict nineteenth-century warehouse in the heart of a newly developed area of the city, The Mailbox, popular for its 'city living' apartments that now pervade Birmingham. The warehouse, in its raw and grubby state, counteracted the use of clean materials and polished surfaces; the work managed to recall the origins of loft living, whilst offering suggestions for alternative living. As such, it demonstrated how a place embodies a number of histories that form part of the material and context. Rather than offer a transformation of the original site, the artist created a free-standing installation, an inhabitable sculpture that transformed its meaning from factory to futuristic living space, the clutter of former employment replaced by the intimacy of personal space.

Much of Ikon's off-site work embodies a participatory engagement and marks the passage of time through traces of production, thus stressing its place in the real world. Time is measured out in gestures corresponding to the comings and goings of everyday life, reminders that all is temporary and mutable. The projects often occur as fleeting gestures and performative actions. These are manifested as much in natural phenomena as in common human-made or urban contexts.

Continuing her series of meteorite projects, Cornelia Parker launched a spectacular firework display from the roof of Birmingham's landmark Rotunda building – *Meteorite Lands in Birmingham's Bull Ring*. The pyrotechnic mixture on this occasion involved a pulverised meteorite. Having already fallen to earth once, in China in the sixteenth century, its combustion repeated the final stage of a cosmic journey, a dazzling meteorite shower over Birmingham's Bull Ring market. Passers-by and those who had come deliberately to witness it shared the experience. There are modes of artistic practice even more transient, artists' fleeting gestures that cannot be collected or stored, except in memory. This notion of myth continues through collective experience, which in turn becomes hearsay absorbed into a public consciousness and also a testimonial of something passing.

Alternatively, Japanese artist Shigenobu Yoshida's ephemeral work involves a participatory element. In a series of holiday workshops with children and community groups Yoshida worked with participants to teach them how to make rainbows, simply with the combination of water, a mirror and sunlight. The results were seemingly 'ordinary miracles'. The project, entitled *Gathering Rainbows*, posits the possibility of inviting the viewer to be a participant in art and nature and inviting nature to make the work itself. Yoshida creates an intervention in nature through his use of unstable and viscous materials such as water and sunlight. The inevitable shifting puts the emphasis on the process of the materials rather than the process of the maker. *Gathering Rainbows* presents the concepts of impermanence, change and destruction, and is thus making a political statement. Working directly with children, Yoshida's work acknowledges that wonder and learning are tied by suddenness and by the moment of first seeing. By courting the unexpected, the everyday is made beautiful and appears suddenly – made even more precious, it seems, in an assertively urban environment.

This project is by its very nature democratic, suggesting that anyone can carry out this simple activity. Inherent in the work is a mutual and shared experience fostered by the artist, who steps back to allow the participant to take control of the experience, thus dispelling the myth of artist as genius. These activities contribute to erasing the boundaries between art and life and replace the act of passivity with participation.

What most of these projects share is their ability to inspire unexpected emotions in the urban experience. Humour, wonder, delight and awe are fed into the collective experience of the city that still struggles to shrug off an image of car-filled, concrete oppression. On all levels, from creative participation to accidental discovery, off-site allows us to make art relevant by making it integral to existence, where a passing witness of Parker's 'meteor' or the child splitting light to make a rainbow is allowed to dream freely. Art is thus entwined with everyday life and 'points (without judging) to those repeated actions, those most travelled journeys, those most inhabited spaces that make up, literally the day-to-day. This is the landscape closest to us, the world most immediately met' (Highmore 2002: 8).

Chapter 9

Merge

Graham Gussin and Nigel Prince

Fragments of ideas and thoughts come to the fore when moving. Being mobile somehow allows fluidity to establish connections to all kinds of places. Recollections of travelling along

or does it resist our perception; we only experience it, as Walter Benjamin says, through distraction, a collection of moods and systems which affect our memory. 'One of the key

are superimpositions of planning and projection. In various conceptualisations of what it means to navigate and inhabit the city, the impact of space is posited on shifting sensations

the emphasis has shifted from intention to use, as Jonathan Raban noted in his prescient exploration of the "soft" elements of cityspace – "the city invites you to remake it."'[1] It feels

this road for nearly 20 years. I've been thinking about how we understand places, so the architecture becomes invisible. Despite our everyday experience of it, is it through familiarity

assumptions of writing about cities and urban experience in the twentieth century has been that they are causative of, or constructed by the neurotic tendencies of the subject – that they

and moods – not what is there but what is supplied or projected – markers of past experiences in which the pedestrian becomes an avatar of hopeful or anxious presence. Increasingly

and looks different today, but then again it feels and looks different every time I travel along this part of the road. I wonder if something, albeit imperceptible, has changed. Maybe

I'm not remembering it correctly, but that large cinema complex wasn't around last time I came along here and also that new shopping complex. Then again, maybe I just didn't

one town and driven through another, perhaps even two or three. The conurbation sprawl just keeps on going, its boundaries fluid, its end never in sight.' As Paul Barker has

probably the ones who feel they have 'arrived'. Now anxiety creeps in, their positions defined but open. Moving on, not knowing when to stop, what to leave behind, what to leave

since it may be that only ruins express a fact completely.'³ 'I am convinced that the future is lost somewhere in the dumps of the non-historical past; it is in yesterday's newspapers,

notice. *The cement collar stranglehold that the ring road established is evaporating. The centre seems to be creeping outward. You can travel for miles and not realize that you've left*

commented in relation to the growth of malls and "edge cities", people like to stop change at the point which benefits them most.'[2] The constituencies who govern these decisions are

standing. What are the things which can be retained, which signal to us clues about the past, present and the future? 'But the question of the fragment in architecture is very important

in the jejune advertisements of science-fiction movies, in the false mirror of rejected dreams.'[4] 24 May 1972. This was its first incarnation; what a symbol of optimism, of forward

thinking. A structure that seemed to embody the opportunity to attain a speed whereby time might be arrested, that we might finally achieve a sense of now, to arrive at the present

communication. Then there's recollection and memory. Through this our travelling continues, from the realms of physical change to the emotional and mental states that by their nature

They always had been and always would be the same. But the universe is now thought to have been born in a primordial explosion some fifteen billion years ago and to have been

history may be more widely self-announcing. Berlin … modern, architecturally "new", confesses its earlier devastation in the very "newness" necessitated by that devastation. … Or

that forever eludes us. What are the ways and means that one generation employs to communicate meaning to the next? Tradition, objects left behind, go hand in hand as direct

can be seen to be in flux. 'Until the 1960's, the universe was generally believed by physicists to be eternal; so were the properties of matters and of fields; so were the laws of nature.

growing and evolving ever since.'⁵ From, to. Stop, start. Old, new. Here, there. Here and now. And back again. 'If the war involves a country's total population or its terrain, the

again Paris, architecturally ancient, silver-white and violet-blue, announces in the very integrity of its old streets and buildings (their stately exteriors undisturbed by war except by the

occasional insertion here and there of a plaque to a fallen member of the Resistance) its survival, its capitulation.'⁶ The city has always remained a place for new beginnings –

Issues of identity, security, civic pride, status are all up for consideration and with each successive group in authority, so these issues take on new meaning. Maybe it is about

we will be constantly drawn back to the memories and emotions that are triggered by this place or that, by the things that remain unaltered, by the clues that are in the architecture

that's encrusted with barnacles . . . But every shell we pick up has its histories, and you certainly don't choose those histories. . . .You have to account for the encrustations and the

both literal and metaphorical. Places to disappear into and places that disappear from view. It may be a biological destiny to keep moving, keep changing, but to what end?

feeling at home, or whatever that could mean. Is the other man's grass greener, or is it a case of altering the perceived mistakes of earlier generations? For all that things change,

or spaces yet to be reconsidered. The porosity of the new seeping into the old only partially resisted. 'I imagine a historical person as being somehow like a hermit crab

inertias, just as you have to remain accountable to each other through learning how to remember, if you will, the barnacles you're carrying.'[7]

Notes

1 Barry Curtis and Claire Pajaczkowska, 'Location Envy', in D. Blamey (ed.) *Here, There, Elsewhere: Dialogues on location and mobility*, London: Open Editions, 2002, pp. 23–4.

2 Ibid., p. 24.

3 Aldo Rossi, *A Scientific Autobiography*, trans. Lawrence Venuti, Cambridge, MA. and London: Oppositions Books, MIT Press, 1981, p. 6.

4 Robert Smithson, 'A Tour of the Monuments of Passaic, N.J.' (1967), in *Blasted Allegories: An anthology of writings by contemporary artists*, Cambridge, MA and London: The New Museum/MIT Press, 1987, pp. 78–9.

5 Rupert Sheldrake, *The Presence of the Past: Morphic resonance and the habits of nature*, New York: First Vintage Books Edition, 1988, pp. xvii–xix.

6 Elaine Scarry, *The Body in Pain: The making and unmaking of the world*, Oxford: Oxford University Press, 1985, p. 113.

7 Donna Haraway, 'Cyborgs at Large', an interview with Constance Penley and Andrew Ross, in C. Penley and A. Ross (eds) *Technoculture*, Minneapolis: The University of Minnesota Press, 1991, p. 48.

1
Aerial view of Birmingham, 2000. Photo Tom Merilion

2
Reuben Colley, *Skyline*, water colour, 2001

3
Reuben Colley,
Mailbox at Night,
water colour, 2001

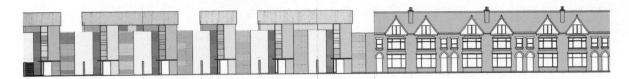

4

Shillam + Smith's design for adaptable housing in Saltley, Birmingham

5

Concept rendering of The Public Building, West Bromwich, showing protruding auditoria, 1999

6

Late development rendering of The Public Building façade, West Bromwich, showing lifting doors, 2002

7

Forward, by Raymond Mason, 1991

8
Katharina Grosse,
Birmingham Central
Library, **2003.**
Photo Chris Webb

9
Tom Merilion, Alpha Tower, 2000

10
**Michael Hallett,
Retaining Wall,
The Bull Ring, 2001**

11
**Richard Harris,
Castle Vale, 1999**

12
**David Rowan,
Demolition, Mass
House Circus, 2002**

13
Ali at the Mailbox, 2003.
Photo Ming de Nasty

15
Reuben Colley, *Traffic,* **2001**

14
Concept rendering
of The Birmingham
Needle, 2003

Chapter 10

Intervening in Birmingham, Reinventing Ourselves

Dave Pollard

As a boy I was allowed to entertain myself by wandering around the derelict houses that populated the inner city landscape of Birmingham in the 1960s. This was over a decade before Urban Renewal, Envelope Schemes and planned regeneration changed the face of Handsworth, Aston and Winson Green. The bomb sites and derelict houses provided not only a playground for me but also an education. Even as a child I understood that the built environment affected the way I felt.

These memories stayed with me as I grew up, and it seemed only natural that I should enter the building trade as a means of making a living because it allowed me to be around the buildings that I had grown up with. However, as a builder I had little access to the process of creating buildings, which was where my real interest lay. In Birmingham I was merely charged with helping to construct them. The creativity went on behind the smoked glass of fashionable architectural practices. It was unlikely, I thought, that I would ever gain the magic letters RIBA after my name.

Because of this, I spent nearly a decade travelling around the world working in countries where the building process was less controlled by authority. I spent time in Africa, the Caribbean and the USA where I came into contact with different ways of approaching the building process. This also included a greater freedom regarding the materials that could be used and the designs that were permitted. In New York, I discovered that there is a much more innovative attitude to departures in interior design and that the boundaries between art and construction are blurred. The old brown-stone houses of Manhattan made a surreal contrast to the skyscrapers and acres of plate glass. Amidst the relentless modernity a good deal of the architecture was much older. The way that the mosaic of different styles had been so beautifully blended together made me think of the possibilities of bringing about a similar fusion in Birmingham.

I arrived back in Birmingham about four years ago. The process of reconstruction and renewal was much further advanced than when I left. Swathes of 1960s' and 1970s' concrete development had been demolished and the city was in the throes of reinventing itself. I can clearly recall thinking that I had to influence this redevelopment of my home town in some way. As I cast around for a way to participate in this process I enrolled at the University of Central England with the intention of doing a degree in Construction Management. However, I soon discovered that the way that I wanted to interact with my built environment could not be realized within this traditional career framework. I wanted a far more dynamic and creative vehicle through which to express myself.

Because I could not find a formal way in to the design process I had to invent my own. Suddenly, I stopped calling what I wanted to do 'building' and instead began to describe it as 'art'. As soon as I did this, I found the reaction of other people to my eccentric ambitions changed

10.1
Dave Pollard: the builder-as-artist, 2001 Photo Julian Bull

dramatically. The unusual plans that I had for the decaying Victorian buildings that I saw all around me were now applauded as innovative and ground-breaking. I was able as an 'artist' to miraculously gain access to a row of five soon-to-be demolished mansions in Handsworth. These properties were owned by a housing association who gave me permission to use them to stage some kind of vaguely defined community arts event. This was the chance I'd been waiting for. So what did I actually want to do with these buildings as my contribution to the rebuilding of Birmingham?

I wanted to provide a stage where not just I but other people could express themselves through a building. For me that might mean adding a parody of a Mondrian painting to a mundane object like scaffolding and attaching it to the front of a Victorian terrace. Or perhaps, taking out a three-storey staircase and constructing a waterfall in the empty stairwell that remained. These kinds of extreme interventions into the buildings represented an explosion of all the repressed creative ambition that had built up over the years. They were not meant to create a serious model for the redevelopment of Birmingham. What they were intended to do was to set a precedent for the democratization of the redesign process of this city.

We titled the Handsworth project *Intervention* and a lot of its energy came from its location. As Julia Ellis noted in her review of the project:

> This 'Art renovation' creates new spatial experiences using materials that also respect the architectural quality and history of the houses. Whilst not an explicitly political act it does stand for renovation in the face of demolition. The historical provenance of the mansions is also relevant in extending the context for the work as this terrace was used as a conduit for immigration from 1930s; firstly as rooming houses for Irish workers and then for Afro-Caribbeans in the 1960s.
>
> (Ellis 2001: 10)

Intervention is a genuine fusion between art and community regeneration away from any established mould; it has the power to capture the imagination and is about people taking control. What amazed me was how many other people flocked to my initiative because they too wanted to interact creatively with their built environment. A group had soon formed around this loose ideal and was christened the Sozo Collective. The need for this kind of organization had obviously lain dormant in a lot of people – in living out my fantasy construction life I was articulating a need in other people's lives.

The Sozo Collective approach is to transcend the prison house of architecture, allowing us to reclaim, transform and reinvent it. We are about the democratization and proletarianization of the redesign of our city. This is not to say that we disregard the expertise and contribution of the established professions whose input is essential for 95 per cent of the redevelopment

House

We make our entrance
tread softly, touch walls
explore the limits of our freedom

We draw the shadow house
into ourselves
paint the dream space
inch into corners, crevices
light the basement
tear up floorboards, cupboards, doors
stoke our own fires

New arrivals on a bright Birmingham day
with hopes and baggage
share rooms, find work
hold parties, write home
huddle together in the cold

The doors are open
new foundations laid
we all live here, now.

Naomi Paul

10.2
Naomi Paul, 'House'. 2001
Photo Julian Bull

of Birmingham. We are simply looking for a meaningful voice for the people who will have to live with the results of the professionals' successes or mistakes. The creative energy that would be released by ordinary people feeling they had a say in the design of their city would be immense and would contribute enormously to Birmingham's ambitions to be a cultural capital.

Under the Sozo approach we can all be empowered to be active in changing our architecture. Moreover, we recognize that this impulse is contagious. Once you've seen it done, this liberates and empowers you to do it again. We have succeeded in achieving a remarkable degree of multicultural involvement in Sozo Collective events. They have been experiments in living as well as experiments in art and architecture. With remarkably little encouragement, people can toil heroically in inhospitable conditions on the building site which most Sozo projects become, and create novel experiences for themselves and for others. We still really don't know why. Maybe it is because they are at last empowered to do something with the physical environment. Maybe it is the camaraderie which develops. Maybe it is because we have been fortunate enough to have some of our projects surrounded by Birmingham's beautiful Victorian architecture and that this

10.3
Dave Pollard, *Totem,* **made from materials retrieved from buildings due to be demolished, 2001**

10.4
Some of the members of the Sozo Collective on site of the *Intervention* project, 2001

resonates with some instinctive need. Maybe because it's fun. It parodies the pre-packaged aesthetics on which we are usually fed via our television screens and magazines. In the politically fashionable spirit of empowerment and social inclusion it offers the architecturally disenfranchised an opportunity to reclaim their heritage.

My hope is that Birmingham as a city will tap into the enormous creative and economic potential inherent in what we have started and support us in establishing a revolution in urban design that actually allows people a chance to participate.

Part III

Imagineering Birmingham

Chapter 11

Birmingham, Photography and Change

Peter James

The transformation of Birmingham's urban landscape has a rich heritage within the visual arts. In the pre-photographic era artists including David Cox, Samuel Lines, J. V. Barber and Thomas Underwood used a range of graphic media including painting, drawing, lithography, and etching to document the changing face of the city.[1] During the last 150 or so years photography has undoubtedly been the most significant medium employed to document and disseminate information about changes in Birmingham's built environment. Architectural subjects were in the forefront of experiments with the new medium from its inception in 1839 and the almost continual building work undertaken in Birmingham has provided rich material for the camera.

During the late nineteenth and early twentieth centuries photography was widely engaged in a series of civic documentary projects in Birmingham. Many of the images made for these projects fall firmly into the canon of civic records taken by the likes of Charles Marville in Paris and Thomas Annan in Glasgow. The photograph was also used as a kind of propaganda tool: to justify and provide evidence of the improvements created by the clearance and redevelopment projects undertaken in the city. City planners hired photographers to verify the extent of poor living conditions so as to bolster the plans for the progressive benefits of rebuilding and regeneration. In more recent times photographs were employed to promote the glossy ideas of perfection presented by architects and planners. Whilst much of this work shared the aims of their nineteenth- and twentieth-century predecessors, many contemporary photographers have produced work that is stylistically individual, resulting in images that are not merely descriptive but subjective and allusive: an artistic response to changes in the city. The scope of what can be represented and the technologies employed to record change have also changed significantly, particularly with the advent of digital photography.

Amongst the first photographs made in Birmingham was a series of views of its principal buildings. These daguerreotypes, made by the enigmatic Frenchman Ste Croix in October 1839, included 'a striking view of the school and the whole of New Street, Christ Church, the hackney coaches and even the scaffold before Warwick House' (Anon. 1839: 5). Within a few years of the public announcement of the invention of the medium the profession of architectural photography was established, as were the majority of techniques and skills required to meaningfully translate a building into a picture. Birmingham's first photographic studio, opened by Henry Whitlock in 1841, was amongst the earliest practitioners of architectural photography in the city. Two albumen prints, views of *Smallbrook Street looking towards Horse Fair,* and of *Dudley Street at the corner of Smallbrook Street from Pershore Street,* each dated May 1867, are amongst the earliest examples of their work in the Central Library's collections. Interestingly, prominent painted notices declaring 'These premises are Not coming down' appear on the walls of commercial premises in both images. It has yet to be established whether these represent some form of restraining guidance for over- exuberant developers or perhaps signs of local resistance to their possible demolition.

One of the earliest attempts to systematically record changes in Birmingham's built environment was founded in 1870. The Birmingham and Midland Institute Archaeological Section (B&MIAS) had as its object the examination, description, and preservation of local antiquities. Members of the B&MIAS noted the great number of buildings that had been pulled down in Birmingham, especially in the centre of town. They therefore decided to commission a local professional photographer, Robert White Thrupp, to make a series of photographs to record the appearance of buildings and streets before they were destroyed. The camera's accuracy, precise delineation of detail and speed of recording made it an invaluable tool for such work. Amongst the surviving images from Thrupp's commission are two albumen prints of Little Charles Street dated *c.* 1870. Taken from two nearby locations on the thoroughfare (from the corner of Newhall Street, looking towards Livery Street and from the corner of Church Street), Thrupp's camera preserved straightforward records of two large areas of ground cleared prior to redevelopment. Two years later Thrupp also recorded the demolition of St Martin's-in-the-Bull Ring, which had fallen into a ruinous state.

Perhaps the largest redevelopment project to impact on the centre of Birmingham during the late nineteenth century was Chamberlain's Improvement Scheme. Between 1830 and 1875, thousands of back-to-back houses were built in the heart of Birmingham to house the town's factory workers and their families. These properties, described by one writer as 'a squalid mass of unsanitary hovels crowded round sunless courts' (Cadbury 1952: 13), became a major social and health problem. Much of the justification for Chamberlain's project therefore came from accounts of the appalling sanitary conditions in these areas. Commenced in the mid-1870s, Chamberlain's plan included the wholesale redevelopment of 93 acres of the town centre and the building of a Parisian-style boulevard, Corporation Street, from New Street to Aston Road. Chamberlain's desire to introduce Parisian-style boulevards in Birmingham owed much to the earlier transformation of Paris by Haussmann. It is not surprising to discover that like their Parisian predecessors, the Committee charged to oversee the Birmingham project also decided to commission a photographer to record the metamorphoses brought about by their scheme. Although there is no evidence to prove that the photographer in question, one James Burgoyne of Small Heath, had seen the work of his French counterpart, Charles Marville, there are many striking similarities in the way the two worked. Each produced unpretentious views with an economy of means and austere forms to record the shops, slums and streets scheduled for demolition. Burgoyne's images of claustrophobic dark, damp courtyards and narrow passageways served to emphasize the squalid living conditions in which many of Birmingham's citizens were then forced to live and stood as testimony to the intent for urban renewal amongst the town's political leaders.

11.1
**James Burgoyne, 86–94 Bull Street,
c. 1870**

In addition to recording the buildings marked for demolition, professional photographers were also engaged to record the major new edifices and institutions that arose in place of the slums on the new streets in Birmingham. For example, shortly after their completion in 1891, the new Assize Courts on Corporation Street, designed by Sir Aston Webb and Ingress Bell and built on land previously occupied by the slums on Lichfield Street, was photographed by the firm of Bedford Lemere & Co. Founded in 1861, the company were acknowledged as being amongst the first to perceive and exploit the growing market for photographs of the new municipal buildings that were transforming the Victorian urban scene. They were therefore the photographers of choice for many of the leading firms of British architects. Bedford Lemere's photographs of the Law Courts bear all the hallmarks which helped them create their professional reputation: the application of meticulous craftsmanship and expertise in executing their commissions, the use of sharp definition of overall form, the absence of dramatic lighting, and the selection of camera positions to show as much of a building as possible on one plate rather than for pictorial effect. The success of Bedford Lemere & Co. highlighted the way in which architectural photography had become the preserve of specialist professionals and also led to the growth of provincial firms such as Thomas Lewis in Birmingham.

In the early years of the twentieth century the issues relating to poor housing stock in the centre of Birmingham continued to exercise the minds of many. In 1901, mounting evidence linking poor housing to ill health and high mortality rates led the city's Housing Committee to establish a policy of 'slum patching'. Instead of sweeping away slum housing and building new properties, sanitary and drainage defects were remedied, damp courses put in, and repairs made to windows, roofs, floors and walls of existing properties. A policy of limited demolition was also carried out to open up courtyards to light and air. In 1904 the Housing Committee engaged J. C. Richards to photograph slum properties in order to assist the evaluation of whether they were suitable for renovation or demolition. Given the growing specialization in architectural photography Richards was an interesting choice for this work. He was by trade a professional artist in stained glass who had taken up photography in 1890, joining both the Birmingham Photographic Society and the Royal Photographic Society. Richards was primarily known as a photographer for his portraiture, figure studies and book on the gum-bichromate process. Many of Richard's images are reminiscent of those taken by Burgoyne in the previous century. In some instances, as if to emphasize the health and sanitation problems associated with this housing stock, Richards' compositions included the public health notices outlining precautions against diarrhoea posted on the doors of slum properties. His detailed documentation process appears to have eventually traced the whole course of the project, recording the shabby run-down housing, the patching process and the completed results with the happy residents outside their refurbished properties.

11.2
J. C. Richards, 21 and 22 William Henry Street, 1905

A different solution to the problems of inner-city housing was developed in the years either side of the Second World War: the construction of new municipal estates on the outskirts of the city. In 1935 the Bournville Village Trust (BVT) inaugurated a programme of research into housing in Birmingham, its relation to industry and the development of the surrounding region. Their findings were collated in an illustrated book, *When We Build Again*, published in 1941 (Bournville Village Trust 1941), and a film of the same name released in 1943. *When We Build Again* was just one of many photographically illustrated books and articles published around this time that sought to address the issues of the living conditions of the working classes and post-war reconstruction. In this context photography was consciously engaged as a journalistic weapon to promote causes and affect conditions. Much of the inspiration for this use of photography came from contemporary illustrated magazines such as *Picture Post*, which had itself published numerous features on the problems of slums and reconstruction. The use of images within publications like *When We Build Again* therefore followed the structure of small photographic essays that, through the careful sequencing and juxtaposition of images and text, made the case for new solutions to old problems.

In addition to adopting the design styles of the popular illustrated press, the BVT also chose to engage a photographer who had published work on the London slums in *Picture Post*: Bill Brandt. Between 1939 and 1943,

Brandt made a comparative study of the living conditions in and around slum housing in the city centre and the new estates built on the outskirts of the city. Some of these were published in *When We Build Again*, and others in later, smaller volumes entitled *Changing Britain: Illustrating the Industrial Revolution* and *Our Birmingham,* both published in 1943. Although none of the Brandt images reproduced in these publications appears to have survived (in Birmingham collections), the BVT Trust Archive includes a remarkable series of some 70 Roliflex negatives and contact prints by Brandt, which were undoubtedly part of the same commission. A careful study of these images reveals the way in which Brandt broke with earlier documentary traditions in creating what have subsequently become described as 'documentary fictions' to fulfil the brief of his commissioning agents. Brandt carefully arranges figures and elements within his pictures, shoots 'day for night' and utilizes dramatic artificial lighting effects in his images. Taking a series of signifiers – light, space, the preparation and consumption of food, sleeping quarters, play areas for children and the proximity to shops and work – he accentuated the contrast between the old (negative) and new (positive) aspects of each type of housing stock, so as to drive home the argument for the forms of redevelopment proposed by the BVT amongst others.

In the second half of the twentieth century photography was increasingly employed as a means of actively promoting such change. One

11.3
Model for the Duddeston and Nechells Redevelopment Scheme, *c.* **1950s**

notable form of imagery that resulted from this process was photographs of the three-dimensional models planners and developers increasingly used to promote their proposed redevelopment schemes. Thus, when in 1944 the City Council approved a grandiose scheme by the architect William Haywood (which included a central parade ground surrounded by formal gardens, office blocks, a new City Hall, a planetarium and buildings for a library, museum and art gallery), the planners commissioned a series of photographs of the designer's model to help project their vision of the future. The practice of photographing architectural models was repeated on a whole series of subsequent projects including the Duddeston and Nechells Redevelopment Scheme of the 1950s, the City Architect's Department's revised plans for the Civic Centre launched in 1955, the Aston Expressway (opened in 1972), the Post Office Tower (completed in 1966) and the Library (opened in 1975).

One such image, of a model of Birmingham Civic Centre, was also amongst the many illustrations to Paul S. Cadbury's volume *Birmingham – Fifty Years On,* published in 1952. Like its predecessors, this book was laden with photographic images (often set in juxtaposition to prospects of the city from the eighteenth and early-nineteenth century), maps, photographs of models, and drawings showing street scenes, and building and transport systems in the imagined city of 2002. Cadbury's book sought to show Birmingham past, present and future within the confines of a single volume. In many respects the design and content of his book simply followed a pattern established by groups with which Cadbury was associated, including the Bournville Village Trust and the West Midlands Planning Group. In 1948 the latter organization published the landmark work *Conurbation: A Planning Survey of Birmingham and the Black Country.* The book is remarkable not only for the breadth and depth of its research and its significant role in the development of town planning, but also for its use of photographic imagery. Many of the subjects described, such as factories and housing, simply drew upon

11.4
Model for the Proposed Civic Centre, approved by the City Council, but not implemented, 1944

established formats such as the use of single or sequences of juxtaposed black and white images. However, it was in the use of constructed panoramas in the representation of the 'Character' or topographical context of the conurbation, and in the remarkable sequence of photographs taken through the window of a train on a journey from Birmingham to Wolverhampton that the creative use of photographic imagery is most striking.[2]

Throughout the period between 1945 and 1980, Birmingham city centre underwent enormous change. To many it seemed that the city was just one big building site. Old buildings were being pulled down, footpaths re-routed, streets diverted and new buildings erected at a phenomenal rate. The confidence exuded in this period was harnessed in attempts to create a totally new type of urban future. As in the previous century, the past was seen an obstruction on the road to the future and comprehensive redevelopment swept away a worn-out pattern and replaced it with a new one that represented modernity and progress. Many of the buildings which have now achieved landmark status in the city, either through popular affection, as in the case of the Rotunda, or by official sanction as in the case of the listing of the Signal Box, were built during this period. This was also the period in which the Inner Ring Road, or 'concrete collar' as it became known, was built around the city.

One of the largest and most significant regeneration projects of this period was the building of the Bull Ring and the Rotunda. The redevelopment process was recorded throughout by a range of professional photographers, including those working for the architects James A. Roberts Associates, the construction company J. Laing and Sons, and the city's Public Works Department. This was also the period in which the plans and foundations were laid for major new buildings in the heart of the city. Here again official photographers were engaged to record the construction process, but they were by no means the only ones documenting changes in the city. Throughout the 1960s and 1970s an amateur photographer, Derek Fairbrother, recorded the demolition and subsequent construction at the sites of twenty key developments in the city. These included the Bull Ring, Birmingham Central Library and the International Convention Centre. Working from carefully selected vantage points, Fairbrother took a series of photographs from the same position at regular intervals throughout the entire process. He then collated his prints into strips that unravel as time-lapse sequences. He intended to film these sequences so that work occurring over a period of years would be condensed into a few minutes. Interestingly, precisely the same process has been undertaken by the developers of the new Bull Ring – however, this time using modern remote digital cameras fixed to the roof of the Rotunda.

Whilst some were simply recording the process of change, other photographers were using their cameras to question the legacy of regeneration and redevelopment in the post-war period. The exhibition *Imagining the City* (1986), compiled by researcher Jude Bloomfield and photographer Roy

Peters and designed by Brian Homer, first shown at the Triangle Gallery in Birmingham, reflected upon the redevelopment of the city between 1941 and 1971. It examined issues such as the politics of town planning, the legacy of the Second World War, the dream of the 'garden city', and the eventual triumph of civil rather than social engineering. The exhibition comprised three sections: archive material drawn from sources such as *Picture Post* and Mass Observation; a series of portraits of notable and influential figures; and a series of new cityscapes which presented Birmingham as the archetypal urban landscape. As one reviewer noted:

> The exhibition demonstrates that social engineering is too important to be left to the planners and politicians. It is a salutary reminder to architects and engineers of what to avoid in the more enlightened eighties. It is essential viewing for all involved in planning and caring for our cities. . . . The nineteenth century visionary and politician Joseph Chamberlain would turn in his grave.
>
> (Hallett 1986: 1369)

(See colour plate 9) In 2000, another project adopted a reflective and questioning approach examining the structure and built environment of the city. Using a traditional architectural lens, experimenting with variable focus and employing an ink jet printer to gain the desired colour saturation for his prints, Tom Merilion created a series of images that evoke the visual feel of the models from which the buildings featured evolved. Merilion's project, entitled *Concrete Dreams*, sought to encourage the viewer to question accepted notions of scale, planning, aesthetics, architecture and beauty. (See colour plate 1) Pushing his experimentation even further, Merilion also produced a series of three-dimensional stereoscopic images, using imaging software to give images the feel and colour palette of the postcards of the 1960s and 1970s. The photographs offer the viewer the opportunity to take the role of planner and rearrange the blocks once again to create one's own concrete dream of Birmingham. Merilion's colour-saturated, small-scale prints and stereoscopic transparencies explored the edifices that represent the personal and architectural landmarks of his youth: the Rotunda, the Bull Ring, Spaghetti Junction, the Post Office Tower, Alpha Tower and Central Library. Once held in the same civic esteem as the Town Hall, Victoria Law Courts and Museum and Art Gallery – built in the previous century – these buildings graced postcards serving as a testament to the city's civic motto: *Forward*. In more recent years some of these same buildings have come to represent the shift in public confidence about the developments of the 1960s.

One of the central subjects of Merilion's project, the Bull Ring, the very image of the confidence of the modern world when new, eventually became viewed along with other plans and developments of that generation as aberrations. Plans to transform the Bull Ring have recently resulted in the largest city centre retail-led development project in Europe.

At the heart of this project will be a new landmark building, the Selfridges store designed by Future Systems. The New Bull Ring is regenerating over 40 acres of land in the centre of Birmingham. Adjacent to this major programme of work is Eastside, an area earmarked for a regeneration initiative that will include a new City Park, a Learning Quarter – which will be home to a new City of Birmingham Library – and Millennium Point, which is the base for a Discovery Centre, a Technology Innovation Centre, the University of the First Age and a new IMAX cinema. Whereas the planners and developers of the past used photographs of models to promote their projects, the web sites and promotional literature of modern-day planners and architects rely heavily on computer-generated images to project impressions of their completed projects.

Nevertheless, alongside the modern there is still room for the more traditional forms of documentation to record the ongoing process of change. Luke Unsworth, a photographer whose work is firmly rooted in the traditions of reportage photography, has been working to 'tell the story' of the development of the Bull Ring in monochromatic images until its completion in 2003. Unsworth's approach to forming a creative narrative around this project is to produce work that gets in amongst the changes to both the physical and social landscape of the area. In particular, Unsworth has chosen to focus on the human dimension of this story and to record the people whom the changes most directly affect: the traders and shoppers who have been the backbone of the Bull Ring for generations gone by.

A completely different approach to the same subject has been adopted by Michael Hallett. Using a combination of a digital camera and traditional film negatives, in 2001 Hallett began making a series of constructed panoramas of the redevelopment of the Bull Ring. Hallett's image-making referenced the historical form of the photographic panorama and the more recent construction techniques of David Hockney's process of creating 'joiners'. (See colour plate 10) However, instead of pasting together the physical objects themselves, Hallett rebuilt and reworked his images on computer to create new master files. As the building work progressed, Hallett's approach to taking and reworking his images also altered. It began with five image, 180° panoramas and evolved into 360° panoramas and images made up from as many as 35 separate images. Hallett eventually dispensed with the digital camera as a tool for making panoramas, using it instead to capture single images that complemented or extended the narrative of his constructed images. In addition to recording the construction work itself, Hallett also turned his camera to the spectacle of consumerism that was and still remains at the heart of the Bull Ring.

Hallett's adoption of the panoramic format and composite imaging is an attempt to expand the conventional camera's limited field of view. Other photographers working in the city have found different ways of expanding the camera's vision without such interventions and manipulation. In 2000 John Davies chose to photograph the city from raised viewpoints. In so doing

he made an extraordinary series of seemingly detached yet intricately designed precise, detailed views of the open spaces which attract people in the city. Davies' large prints and chosen position allow the viewer a privileged viewpoint, laying out the city as if it were on a drawing board. Ian Jeffrey suggests that if Davies' pictures have any historical affinities 'it is with the great panoramic pictures of the 1870s, especially with Eadweard Muybridge's famous survey of San Francisco taken in 1878' (Jeffrey 2001: 64). Davies' Birmingham photographs are part of a larger project photographing the major industrial and post-industrial cities of Britain including Newcastle, Manchester, Swansea, Glasgow, Belfast and London. His aim is to produce a coherent series of images of individual cities and metropolitan areas which reflect the positive achievements and reality within these continually changing urban centres. Although expressing a 'wish to remain objective in this documentary work', Davies recognizes that it has become increasingly important 'to question as well as celebrate our collective responsibility in shaping the environments in which we live' (James 2001: 13).

Thus far, regeneration and the photographic responses to this process have largely been considered on the macro level of large-scale developments within the city. In contrast, Helen Sweeting's personal project seeks to explore some of the human issues around the identity that an environment develops in relation to the people or persons that occupy it on a much smaller scale. In September 2000 Sweeting's grandmother Rene died. She was 90 years old and had lived on the same road in Handsworth, Birmingham, all of her life, moving ten houses away from her parents upon her marriage 60 years ago. Following her death Sweeting started photographing her home, a space that evoked many personal memories for her and her family. Sweeting's goal was to capture her grandmother's essence within these walls – her private space, creating one final portrait of her, a portrait-in-absentia. She photographed the home before the possessions, the remnants of her grandmother's existence, were removed and when her family sold the house she befriended the new owners, a Muslim family that knew her grandmother. On subsequent returns to the house she interpreted its reduction to an empty shell, stripped to its brickwork in preparation for its rejuvenation. New rooms and corridors have since been created and decorated and with the transformation recently completed, the new family have moved in. Sweeting's images record the metamorphosis and regeneration of this house, its changing identity, as a new family creates their own home, a new presence and influence within these walls.

Another contemporary photographer dealing with similar issues is Richard Harris. His *Utopias* series, made in 1999, explored the abandoned domestic spaces of 1960s' council flats on the Castle Vale Estate, prior to their recent demolition and the construction of new homes for the former residents. Originally created as a saviour from the Victorian and Edwardian slums, over time Castle Vale fell into disrepair and gained a bad reputation.

Harris's images capture the residual evidence of the human presence in the flats – the wallpaper and fittings that retain the memories and experiences of the former residents – and explore the gaps between the utopian vision that created the estate and the real-life experiences of those who lived in them. (See colour plate 11) To complete the body of work Harris subsequently photographed many of the former residents of tower blocks in Castle Vale in the new houses created for them on the estate. Here again, Harris explores the personalization of living spaces and poses questions as to whether these new homes and their residents will eventually suffer the same fate as their predecessors.[3]

David Rowan is another photographer who is interested in the ways in which the urban environment and changes to that environment affect the lives of ordinary people. Rowan's work, *Pacha Kuti* (the word Pacha in the Inca language means Earth, or time; Kuti means turn upside down or to set things right) explores another legacy of the 1960s, the subways and underpasses, the underground car parks and walkways that are now considered to be failures in terms of viable city living. The construction of the ring road in the 1960s created the need for underpasses which restricted pedestrians' access and ability to locate themselves within their city. The pedestrian was subjugated to the car: the world was turned upside down. Originally seen as safe, clean and efficient facilities, they quickly became dirty, dangerous, and impracticable. The massive changes that are taking place in the city, with pedestrianization reclaiming the streets for the people and the demise of the ring road symbolized in the demolition of Mass House Circus, provide Rowan with ample subject matter through which to explore these ideas. (See colour plate 12) Rowan's documentary work around these sites, including his detailed work recording the demolition of Mass House Circus, are used as a point of departure for abstraction through the use of both analog and digital processes. Like Merilion, Rowan creates images that seek to suggest what the visionaries of the 1960s were aiming at but never achieved. He creates video and still images of subjects that do not exist in reality, but ones that nevertheless reveal an aesthetic link between his perspectives and the ideals of the planners. As with the redevelopment and regeneration of the city itself, this is work in progress.

Notes

1   From time to time the work of these artists was published in illustrated books such as *The Buildings of Birmingham, Past and Present, Sketched and Described* (1866). This particular volume consisted of lithographed drawings, plans, prospects and panoramic views with accompanying texts describing 'buildings removed during the last half century, or threatened during the next few years' (Sackett 1866: 2).

2   Staff at the Centre for Urban and Regional Studies at the University of Birmingham are currently producing a contemporary response to this key post-war planning initiative, which revisits the realities of the conurbation as seen in 1948 and reviews the planners' vision for the conurbation fifty years on. Nick Hedges, a Midlands documentary photographer

who has published and exhibited work on the changing social and industrial landscape of the region, has been commissioned to produce a new body of colour work to illustrate the book.

3   Harris recently started work on a new project documenting the restoration of the only remaining examples of back-to-back housing in Birmingham. Built from 1802 to 1831, the back-to-back houses of Inge and Hurst Street will provide a unique look into the lives of its former residents and provide a vehicle for revealing the history of urban working-class life over a period of 150 years. In this new work Harris develops his interest in how people operate and organize domestic spaces, revolving especially around abandoned properties.

Chapter 12

Take Me Higher
Birmingham and Cinema

Justin Edgar

One drizzly evening in October 2001, I walked up a red carpet outside the UGC cinema on Broad Street in Birmingham. People walked past heading back to the suburbs after work, bewildered as to why they had to step over a red carpet and what exactly was going on. Inside the cinema a gang of bemused teenagers in tracksuits were buying tickets for *American Pie 2*. I stared up at the cinema, which was covered in posters for *Large* – my first film. The first film ever to be shot and set entirely in Birmingham. With no incentive given to shoot locally and all of the finance coming from outside of the region, we spent one million pounds of the budget in the city. It was conceived as a proudly regional film with locations including the newly redeveloped Brindleyplace and Broad Street.

I knew the premiere was not going well – by the time the actors arrived, the local press had all gone home for tea. There was an inexplicable air of indifference towards this new British film being shot and released in the city. None of the local papers covered the premiere, only nationals. *Large* was given a limited theatrical release in Birmingham and audiences stayed away in their droves. It did not help that, according to box office figures, the people of Birmingham do not go to the cinema. It has some of the lowest cinema admissions of any major city in Europe. Nor did it help that the local television news programme *Midlands Today* branded *Large* 'controversial' because they felt it made Birmingham people look stupid.

In his review of *Felicia's Journey* in the *Observer*, film critic Philip French comments: 'This week sees that most unusual of things: a feature film set in Birmingham' (French 1999). Why would anyone want to make a film set in Birmingham? Cinematic representations of the city make up a short and not often distinguished list. Probably the best-known films to be shot in the city were not even set here. For example, scenes from Alan Clarke's football hooligan drama *The Firm* (1988) were shot in the city centre. *Brassed Off*'s (1996) climax at the Royal Albert Hall was actually filmed in Birmingham Town Hall. The city occupies a kind of hinterland between kitchen sink depictions of the north and the period dramas of the south. It seems ironic that although Birmingham was the town where nineteenth-century plastics pioneer Josiah Parkes invented celluloid, so little of it has been shot here.

I set my feature film in Birmingham because I was inspired by the cinematic potential of the city and by the humour and wit of the people I grew up amongst. Birmingham is an amazing-looking city. It is very American in layout and from the air Spaghetti Junction looks more like the freeway system of Los Angeles than urban England. It is easy to see this robust concrete city in cinematic terms; it lends itself to a cinematic imagination. I want to comment here on some cinematic representations of Birmingham and speculate on what I see as recurrent themes.

The first major feature film to showcase Birmingham's post-war redevelopment was *Take Me High* (1973, also known as *Hot Property*), starring Cliff Richard, and the only feature of television director David Askey and television writer Christopher Penfold. Richard plays Tim Matthews, a merchant banker who is initially annoyed to be posted to Birmingham until he gets to grips with the lively locals, falls for a local restaurateur and teams up with her to launch the Brumburger, a revolutionary new fast-food concept. At the same time, Tim acts as a mediator between a working-class left-wing city councillor and a local property developer to broker a massive city redevelopment deal. As a reward for being successful, he is offered a posting in New York, but turns down the offer of a Manhattan apartment to stay on his canal barge. The film celebrates regionality and culminates in a festival of local pride as the Brumburger is launched amidst a blaze of publicity on New Street. In *Take Me High* buildings such as the Alpha Tower and the Rotunda still look gleamingly new and Askey clearly uses them in contrast to the old-fashioned working-class environment where Tim decides to lodge – a narrowboat moored at Gas Street Basin. Scant regard is shown for the representation of the locals as casting was done in London and many of the working-class characters have cockney accents. Nonetheless, *Take Me High* was the first Birmingham film of mainstream note and set a precedent for making fiercely regional, brashly kitsch films in the city.

Urban horror is a genre several film-makers have used in depictions of Birmingham. In the mid-1980s Dirk Campbell and Mycal Miller, editors at local television station Central on Broad Street, met *Evil Dead* director Sam Raimi and decided to make a Birmingham-based comic splatter movie of their own. It was entitled *I Bought a Vampire Motorcycle* (1989) and was made with the cast and crew of the Central drama series *Boon*. Director Campbell traded on the heritage of the locally produced Norton Motorcycles and of Birmingham as a centre for heavy metal music. He was keen to keep the film firmly rooted in the city, but using very different locations to *Take Me High*:

I wanted the film to have the look of a serious horror movie, a dark gritty realistic look that used the decaying back streets of Birmingham, so there's nothing that jumps out at you to tell you it's a comedy.[1]

A more recent example of the genre was produced in 1997 when Kings Heath-based Dead Good Film Company (bolstered by the cult success of their short *Rhinobitch*) unleashed their first feature, *Demagogue*. Co-directed by sound designer Tom Lawes and BBC editor Adam Trotman, *Demagogue* is a splatter movie about a psychic baby used to contact violent aliens. It was shot on video in Kings Heath and had a successful UK video release, also selling throughout the world. Like *I Bought a Vampire Motorcycle*, it uses suburban Birmingham as a backdrop for splatter-antics and brash gross-out humour. Andrew Spencer's digital feature *Dark Eyes* (2001) is an altogether more psychological foray into Birmingham horror, this time using the location of Erdington in the north of the city.

Social tensions in inner Birmingham have provided a stimulus and material for some notable films. Ian Eames (who now works in Hollywood on television shows such as *The Invisible Man*) was born in Birmingham and directed *Knights and Emeralds* (1986) in the city. The story revolves around rivalry between West Midlands marching bands. Racial tensions arise when a white boy has a relationship with a black girl. In the wake of the tensions and cynicism towards the police force following the Handsworth Riots of 1985, racial politics became another theme in Birmingham cinema. In 1986 probably the most successful and enduring film ever made in Birmingham, John Akomfrah's *Handsworth Songs*, was made by the Black Audio Film Collective in Handsworth. It is a dizzying visual collage, an experimental documentary interweaving interviews, archive footage of the city and rostrum camera to put the viewer in the midst of the riots. The Victorian suburban houses of Handsworth become a burning backdrop for the violent confrontations. *Handsworth Songs* points the finger of blame squarely at the media and its biased depictions of black youth. The following year, Johnnie Turpie directed *Out of Order*. Like *Handsworth Songs*, its subject was alienated inner city youth clashing with the police. Although actually set in Telford, it was produced by the now defunct Birmingham Film and Video Workshop and was again very regional in outlook, theme and content.

Oscar-nominated director Atom Egoyan came to Birmingham in 1998 to shoot parts of his ode to Hitchcock, *Felicia's Journey* (1999). It was based on William Trevor's novel, set in an unnamed Midlands industrial town. The film put Birmingham on the world stage at Cannes in 1999, where it screened in competition and very nearly won the Palm d'Or. Canadian cinematographer Paul Sarrossy shoots Birmingham like an intimidating concrete maze. *Felicia's Journey* shows some of the same locations as *Take Me High*, twenty-five years on, decaying and dirty. The once gleaming concrete has turned black. The city centre is photographed from below and at oblique angles. Further out of town, gasometers loom in the distance. Jonathan Romney noted in his review:

> *Felicia's Journey* highlights a zone of life generally ignored in British film – the marginal landscapes of suburbia and industrial estates, photographed in stark panorama by Paul Sarrossy. It's a truism to say that foreign directors bring a sharper, stranger look to British scenery.
>
> (Romney 1999)

In one shot Hilditch drives Felicia around searching for her boyfriend. Hilditch's Morris Minor appears like a tiny beetle or insect, dwarfed by massive cooling towers. This is an image loaded with pertinence to Birmingham as the two lost souls are subjugated to the vast, inhuman industrial landscape of the city.

Where Trevor's novel succeeds, Egoyan's film fails. Trevor builds the tension, making the audience believe that Hilditch is a serial killer who is going to murder Felicia, like the other various 'lost girls' he has befriended. He turns out to be merely a sad, emotionally inadequate lost soul, destroyed by his loneliness. In the film, though, Hilditch does become a serial killer, bent on killing Felicia and then burying her in the garden. Part of Birmingham's identity is its mundanity. Serial killers do not belong in Birmingham, they belong in Hollywood. An even more unbelievable innovation of the film was making Hilditch the son of a Fanny Craddock-style 1950s' television chef. A serial killer in Birmingham? Perhaps. But a 1950s' television chef seems highly unlikely. Fanny Craddock would never have lived in Birmingham.

But Mr Peach would have. Ricky Tomlinson had a small part in *Out of Order* and went on to play the lead in *Nasty Neighbours* (1999). His rumbustiousness seems perfectly suited to Birmingham cinema. Debbie Issit adapted the film from her play *Mr Peach* and although the city is not specifically mentioned, most of the film was shot in Birmingham. It is very much a suburban story – set-in-his-ways Mr Peach battles with his new yuppie neighbours – and is firmly rooted in the tradition of kitsch Birminghamana: 'The sexually frustrated wife hits the bottle amid mantilla'd dolls from the Costa Brava – we're not far away from the Donald McGill world of the saucy postcard' (Kemp 2000).

In the late 1990s Birmingham's young people came into the frame again, perhaps reflecting the emerging young film-making talent in the region, perhaps reflecting the new popularity of the city centre as a magnet for young people. Richard Gossage's *Beach Boys* (1999) told the story of two lads who embark on a journey of self-discovery in Brighton – I was line producer on the film, for which Birmingham doubled up as Brighton. Paul Hupfield's *Club* (2002) was a digitally shot feature revolving around the city's club culture. I was inspired by the clubbers of Broad Street to make the short film *Large* (1997), which later became the aforementioned feature of the same name.

12.1
Going around in circles: Laurence (Dominic Coleman) attempts to escape from the Rotunda in *Round,* **2003**

So what are the common themes that emerge from Birmingham's limited cinematic corpus? I think that comedy will always be a dominant force in Birmingham cinema – even the horror films made here tend to have a comic edge. The next major cinematic treatment of Birmingham will be Andy Humphries' *Sex Lives of the Potato Men* (shooting as I am writing this chapter). The script examines a group of potato deliverymen and the sadness of their sexual exploits. It is very funny indeed and firmly rooted in Birminghamana. The city's landscape also has a key role to play in the evolution of a cinematic Birmingham. I shot my latest short film *Round* (2003) in the Rotunda, Birmingham's most iconic building. The building seemed ideally suited to the melancholic nature of a sadly romantic comedy. It may be a scruffy landmark from the outside, but inside the air is one of faded 1970s' glamour. We shot the interiors with wide lenses to accentuate the curves and make it seem like an even more enclosed environment than it is. The empty floors have a peculiar stillness punctuated by the hum of fluorescent lights and a distant buzz of the city thirteen floors below. There is a sense that nothing ever really happens in there. If you walk along one of the long, round corridors, you end up back where you started. The exteriors were shot as major building work was going on all around, yet the Rotunda endures, an indomitable pillar, symbol of the fading modern style that once defined the city, yet still at the centre of its constant evolution.

Note

1   From *I Bought a Vampire Motorcycle* production notes, Dirk Productions, 1990.

Chapter 13

The Altered Eye

The European Capital of Culture Bid and Visual Images of Birmingham

Jane Lutz

In 1999 the European Union agreed to designate one city, annually, as the European Capital of Culture (ECOC) and in 2008 the title will be given to a UK city. Set up in 1985 as the European City of Culture,[1] the year-long cultural event is now a major generator of cultural tourism and Richards (2000: 159) argues that, in addition to its potential as an artistic showcase, its perceived economic, social and environmental benefits are so great that cities fight over it with the intensity usually reserved for the Olympic Games nomination. In 2000, the UK government signalled that it viewed the title as a significant prize and highlighted that 2008 should be seen as an opportunity for the UK title-holder to transform its image: 'The year should mark a lasting change in the city's standing in its own eyes, throughout the UK and on the continent' (DCMS 2000: 4). This is the story of Birmingham's bid. It will explain why the city decided to enter the competition, summarize the bid's content, and tell the tale of how the bidding process intensified debates about the city's cultural image. It will also describe how the Capital of Culture contributed to the visual economy of the city by developing a new set of visual images for marketing purposes. In conclusion there will be a summary of some key issues to emerge from this case study of a culture-led competition.

Birmingham decided to enter the competition for three main reasons. First, the title was a huge opportunity to reposition the outdated and largely negative image of the city and communicate the changes that had been created and were planned via its existing culture-led regeneration strategy. Second, it was a vehicle for cementing and deepening its European

13.1
The Custard Factory, Birmingham,
2003

connections[2] and, third, it was a way of forging improved relationships with its wider region. The bid submitted to the DCMS is in the public domain and is available on the website www.beinbirmingham2008.net. The document is much more than a prospectus for a year-long cultural festival. It attempts to convey how the year could make a distinctive and unique contribution to the vitality and well-being of the city and region. There is a constant emphasis that the bid has grown out of the city's and region's own distinct geographical and historic circumstances and its unique social, cultural and intellectual context. Meetings with a vast number of individuals and organizations influenced the content and the bid includes over 600 projects submitted by individuals and organizations. The bid has six themes that were designed to provide a clear framework around which the programme for 2008 would be shaped. The themes are: The Imaginative and Sustainable City; Connecting the Region; Learning; Creative Individuals, Creative Networks; Diversity as an Essential Asset; and Celebrating Success and Lifting Aspirations. Within the last theme there is a specific 'image' objective: 'To communicate our region's cultural excellence in order to improve internal and external perceptions of both the city and the region'.

The central goal of Birmingham's bid is to nurture the talents and creativity of its people and celebrate the diversity of its cultures. Unlike in previous events (Myerscough 1994), there is not a major focus on using the title to stimulate new infrastructural projects. In fact, Birmingham stressed in its bid that it has, since the 1990s, been a trailblazer for culture-led regeneration in the UK and it has already developed a critical mass of cultural infrastructure – for example, Symphony Hall, the National Indoor Arena, and Birmingham Royal Ballet's performance and rehearsal facilities. However, this shift in cultural planning from an emphasis on 'hard' building-based infrastructure to 'soft' people- and organization-based infrastructure presents challenges for image marketing campaigns. It is much simpler to communicate in visual terms a new set of buildings than it is to convey the activity that may happen within them.

Birmingham has a sound but contested track record in culture-led regeneration that has been noted elsewhere (Barber 2001; Bloomfield and Bianchini 2002; Caffyn and Lutz 1999; Hubbard 1995; Lim 1993; Loftman and Nevin 1994; Lutz and Ryan 1997; Sandercock 2002; Webster 2001). A review of city and regional strategy and policy documents (Birmingham City Council 2001a; 2001b; 2002; Advantage West Midlands 2001; West Midlands Life 2001) reveals that culture in its widest sense[3] is seen as a means of achieving economic, social, and environmental regeneration within the city centre and in peripheral neighbourhoods. Within these documents it is clear that culture is viewed as a vital tool to improve internal and external perceptions of the city and region. It is to discussion of image, the visual aspects of culture and the Capital of Culture competition that we now turn.

Birmingham, like many other post-industrial cities (Kotler *et al.* 1999; Short 1998; Ward 1998), has an image problem[4] of which it is aware and to which it must respond if it is to be seen as a dynamic, attractive cultural city with a high quality of life rather than an ugly and functional former industrial centre. To help develop a successful image marketing strategy policymakers in the city can draw on a rapidly growing body of conceptual and empirical research on image and place-marketing. The power of culture to contribute to regional economic development by meeting the needs of key target markets has been well documented (Florida 2002; Kotler *et al.* 1999; Landry 2000) and culture- and event-led strategies have been widely debated (Bianchini and Parkinson 1993; Evans 2001; Hall 1992; Hughes 1999; Hughes 2000; Judd and Fainstein 1999; Richards 1996; Ward 1998). Aestheticization as a dynamic within cities and the growth of the symbolic cultural economy have been discussed by Zukin (1995).

The Capital of Culture competition and the achievements of previous cities of culture[5] have aroused the interests of individual authors (Wishart 1991) and numerous scholars (Boyle and Hughes 1991; Clohessy 1994; Heikkinen 2000; Hitters 2000; Hopia 2001; Lutz 2003; Myerscough 1992; Richards 2000; Roth and Frank 2000; Sjoholt 1999). One of the key findings from this body of work is that image enhancement was the major benefit sought by previous title-holders. For example, Heikkinen's 'In from the margins: The City of Culture and the image transformation of Helsinki' records in detail how the year's programme was designed to create the image of a geographically peripheral city which had forged a new image and identity as an informational city connected to the heart of Europe and strongly embedded in global communication networks. Wishart gave the title 'Fashioning the future: Glasgow' to her piece and argued that one of the most important legacies of the year was the transformation of the city image from a mean, violent and declining industrial place to a welcoming, cultural and attractive place.

A number of insights have been gained from the wider work on image, culture and marketing and from the specific literature on the Capital of Culture event. It appears that to use culture effectively and sensitively within image marketing it is important to:

- Align marketing activities to a wide set of social, environmental and cultural goals;
- Create a distinctive, authentic and inclusive vision of local culture;
- Understand that place-making must underpin any place-marketing strategy;
- Embrace the notion of difference and diversity within cultural marketing strategies and understand the importance of inter-culturalism as well as multiculturalism;
- Adopt a realistic and long-term strategic market-oriented approach based on a thorough audit of resources;

- Ensure that a partnership approach to planning and implementation is adopted. This should recognize that cities are heterogeneous, complex and dynamic forces where culture is very rarely uncontested;
- Focus on the need to stimulate the creative resources within a city, while acknowledging that catering for the consumption of culture by visitors is important in order to maximize the economic benefits from cultural tourism.

The realization that the visual aspects of culture were crucially important was brought home forcefully at the shortlisting stage[6] of the ECOC competition. There was widespread media coverage of the shortlist announcement with five of the nationals[7] picking up the story. *The Times* and *The Guardian* both accompanied their stories with photographs of the cities' cultural assets. The *Birmingham Post* (the city's daily newspaper) also ran an illustrated story on the other five shortlisted cities and for each of them cited the 'landmark' cultural assets of the city.

Birmingham had good reason to be sensitive about its competitors' cultural landmarks. Immediately after the shortlisted cities were announced, Sir Jeremy Isaacs, the Chair of the panel of judges advising DCMS on the ECOC2008 competition, praised the city's commitment to culture-led regeneration:

> You've got to give a city a credit for what it's done. Birmingham has the best concert hall in Britain and that may be something that other cities envy. Having known the city for several years now from my work at the Royal Opera House with Birmingham Royal Ballet, and knowing the welcome which was extended to the company . . . I am pleased that Birmingham is on the shortlist.

However, in the same interview (Grimley 2002), he also identified a lack of visual identity as a weakness in Birmingham's bid:

> The Birmingham people who came to visit us[8] would know themselves that the city has a very, very solid record of culture to point to. What they might not have is any one defining image of the city that commends it to the world. That is not something the panel can do anything about.

Sir Jeremy had thrown down the gauntlet and challenged the city to overcome its perceived visual identity weakness.

This challenge was an opportunity to bring out into the open criticisms of the city's historical lack of concern over urban design, and lack of effective marketing of its cultural assets. The *Birmingham Post* (*Birmingham Post* 2002) ran a leader on the day after the announcement that picked up on Sir Jeremy's comments. Whilst acknowledging the satisfaction that came with making it through to the shortlist, it also voiced a frustration with what it saw as Birmingham's poor attitude towards the built environment and lack-lustre attempts at commissioning world-class architecture. The city's poor track record was compared with the positive approach of Newcastle/ Gateshead, which were cited as utilizing powerful images of new iconic architecture (the Baltic Mill Art Gallery and the award-winning Millennium Bridge) in order to create a 'wow' factor that had made them the accepted front runners in the race.

Birmingham, it opined, had to learn two important lessons from its competitors. The first was 'that great international cities tend to be recog-nised as such because they have great international-quality architecture. This is a simple fact which Birmingham, happy to accept second-best for far too long, has been surprisingly slow to recognise.' It also chastised the city for its failure to communicate visual images of its good buildings and public spaces within its regenerated city centre: 'The other [lesson] is that when you do come up with powerful, positive images, it's a good idea not to keep them to yourself.' The piece went on to mention specifically that the city's marketers had failed to effectively promote key sites (the Council House and Victoria Square) to the national and international media. The Capital of Culture bidding team did not escape criticism either. Its web site was criticized for failing to showcase images of the city's gem heritage sites. The web site was also lambasted for not adequately conveying, in visual terms, the range and diversity of the city's artistic life.

The bid team had, in fact, been long exercised with the challenge of creating new visual images that it could use to communicate the city's regenerated public realm and dynamic and diverse cultural scene. Before it was attacked for its neglect in this area it had been a long-standing and active partner[9] in a European Union (EU) funded project entitled 'Capitalising on Culture'. The primary aim of the project (Birmingham Arts Marketing 2002: 3) was to highlight, to national and international target markets, the range, diversity and quality of cultural activity in the city and wider region. Amongst its other activities the project commissioned three local photographers to create new imagery of the city that challenged existing preconceptions and positioned the region as a dynamic cultural destination (See colour plate 13). The image attempts to convey a city of movement inhabited by a diverse and youthful population. It shows a young person in the forefront looking out of the frame and the strikingly lit Mailbox building makes up the backdrop. Hence two stories can be told: the first is about the demographic mix of the city and the second is about the physical regeneration through imaginative adaptive reuse of buildings.

After the shortlisting announcement more resources flowed into the bid team's coffers for the purposes of creating new imagery to highlight the city's cultural assets and that of its surrounding region. In early December 2002, the Regional Development Agency, Advantage West Midlands (AWM), launched its Regional Marketing Strategy. Within this there was acknow-ledgement that the bid for the city and the region[10] was an intelligent way to communicate the region's cultural assets and reinforce the reality that cultural-led regeneration made it an attractive place to live, work, invest in and visit. In providing the extra resources, AWM was acting in part on the recommendations of an earlier piece of research (Lutz *et al.* 2002) that it had commissioned into the image of the region as portrayed in the media. The recommendations were that the region should develop a new image bank for the media and that there should be much more use made of the positive cultural icons within the region. AWM's contribution meant that the bid's marketing budget was boosted by an extra £1 million. It has used part of this money to commission two leading photographers, Brian Griffin and Tom Merilion (both of whom have close links to the city), and a local creative business, Seeing the Light, to create a photographic exhibition entitled *The People and the City: A Cultural Portrait of Birmingham.*

Apart from commissioning the photographic exhibition, designed to change the perceptions of Birmingham among key metropolitan cultural and media figures,[11] the bid team was engaged in other activity where imagery and visual aspects of culture were seen as strategically important to the bid's development. The original bid submitted to DCMS contained over 600 projects from organizations and individuals across the city and region. In order to communicate and market this content, it was not practical to promote such a large number of projects. The bid team had to decide on a sample of projects that could illustrate the new cultural assets that would be in place by 2008 and give a flavour of the range and breadth of the 2008 festival programme. One of the most important criteria used to select the sample was a project's potential to provide strong visual images that could be used within marketing campaigns. Thus landmark architectural projects were selected: Lord Rogers' new library, the stunning new Needle video-walled building (see colour plate 14) and the Will Alsop-designed The Public Building. However, the selection was not restricted to architectural projects. For example, it was decided to showcase the Slowfilm project that will transform buildings in the region into giant screens that will time-stretch famous films so they run for 24 hours. The Bhangra Festival was selected because of the visual messages that it conveys about a modern cultural form that was invented in Birmingham and which is due to celebrate its fortieth birthday in 2008. To illustrate the fact that traditional high European culture will be represented, the taster programme of projects included the Rubens portrait exhibition that is planned for venues throughout the city in 2008. The Edible Schoolyard project, nurtured by the Creative Partnership Project in the city, was chosen for the visual potential it had and to capture the excitement of the learning theme within the bid.

The bid team has also created cheap and easy access to powerful professional quality visual images that illustrate the city's cultural assets. It has done this by placing a set of key images on a commercial web site[12] respected by national and international media.

Cultural Competitions: Issues to Consider

High profile cultural events like the ECOC are much coveted because of their power to improve external perceptions and change negative, stereotyped images of places. One of the main reasons Birmingham entered the competition was to shake off its former image as an undistinguished, rather ugly provincial centre of manufacturing. It used the bidding process to assert itself as a dynamic, diverse and culturally rich place that could offer its residents and visitors cultural experiences second to none in Europe. However, the journey towards achieving this shift in image has not been simple or trouble-free. Entering a competition based on cultural assets and focused on publicly articulating cultural aspirations has thrown up some issues that other cities contemplating following this path might want to consider. In Birmingham bidding for the ECOC revealed that:

- Bidding for major cultural prizes can generate all party political and significant local media support. However, this does not mean that all critical debate about cultural policy is suppressed.
- The bid has illustrated the strengths and weaknesses of the city's cultural achievements. The publicity around the competition has been a positive way of conveying the city's track record in cultural investment. However, the city has also had to concede that the judging panel noted its poor record in creating a strong visual identity for itself. The creation of a distinctive visual identity is crucially important for any place that wants to successfully promote itself to outsiders, especially cultural tourists.
- Success breeds success. After the bid had successfully made the shortlist, the major player in funding regional economic development increased its financial support.
- Geography matters when attempting to create powerful and distinctive visual images of places. Geographically, Birmingham is disadvantaged in terms of the cityscape it can use in its visual images because unlike other shortlisted cities (Bristol, Cardiff, Liverpool and Newcastle/Gateshead), it does not have a significant river or waterfront. Its refurbished canal-side is used to illustrate its physical regeneration but its scale does not bear comparison with the other port and riparian cities.
- History and heritage matter. Birmingham lacks the quality and range of heritage buildings and the 'dreaming spires' skyline of Oxford. The past also matters in terms of the legacy left by previous policy decisions. Birmingham is a city that has not until recently had the political will or the artistic vision to commission world-class iconic buildings.
- Time-limited cultural competitions can be useful mechanisms for 'packaging' existing but disparate ideas and moulding them into

a coherent visual story. In Birmingham there were numerous examples of existing lighting, film and video installation projects that used the city's buildings as canvasses.

- Distinctiveness and authenticity are crucially important. Unlike most of the other competing cities, the bid team avoided relying heavily on external consultants to brand the city and determine the content of the bid. The bid team included a local historian whose perspective ensured that the aspirations for 2008 were always rooted in the city's past.
- Bids can stimulate the development of new visual representations of place and celebrate local creative talent.
- Birmingham's vision of using 2008 to develop the creative potential of its people and celebrate its cultural diversity resulted in a much more complex proposition than other bids that took a much more standard festival programming or cultural infrastructure development to the year. It is inherently more difficult to convey this approach in visual terms.

Conclusion

By making shortlist of cities competing to become ECOC, Birmingham can now officially brand itself as one of the six centres of cultural excellence in the UK. Whether or not it finally wins the title in 2008, the experience of bidding will have been a valuable step along the journey of repositioning itself as a leading European cultural city. In the city itself the competition has created widespread awareness of how culture can contribute to physical, social and economic regeneration. On a practical level the bidding process has stimulated the creation and dissemination of new visual images of the city as a cultural place. On a more sobering note, by looking outward to see how it has been judged against its competitors, the city has been forced to realize that there is a pressing need for it to create a powerful and distinctive visual identity for itself. This is something it has yet to achieve. It is a challenge that it must confront if it is to shake off its existing negative, stereotyped images. Only by doing this can it convey the reality of the powerful human and physical cultural assets that it possesses.

Notes

1 Further details of the competition can be found on www.culture.gov.uk. Twelve UK cities entered the competition to become European Capital of Culture in 2008. They were: Belfast, Birmingham, Bradford, Brighton, Bristol, Canterbury, Cardiff, Inverness, Liverpool, Newcastle/Gateshead, Norwich and Oxford.
2 The bid included personal endorsements from leading political figures in six European cities: Barcelona, Copenhagen, Frankfurt, Helsinki, Lyons and Prague.

3   The definition of culture in these strategies and the concept of culture used in the bid document are wide and broadly follow that used by the DCMS (see DCMS 2001). This includes: the performing and visual arts, craft and fashion; media, film, television, video and language; museums, artefacts and design; libraries, literature, writing and publishing; the built heritage, architecture, landscape and archaeology; sports events, facilities and development; parks, open spaces, wildlife habitats, water environment and countryside recreation; children's play, playgrounds and play activities; tourism festivals and attractions; informal leisure pursuits.

4   For the most recent results of research into the image of the city and region, see Lutz *et al.* (2002).

5   From 1998 the title became European Capital of Culture rather than European City of Culture.

6   On 30 October 2002 six cities (Birmingham, Bristol, Cardiff, Liverpool, Newcastle/ Gateshead and Oxford) were shortlisted and designated as Centres of Culture by DCMS.

7   The *Independent*, The *Guardian*, *The Times*, The *Sun* and *Metro*.

8   Part of the selection process was a presentation by the bidding city to the Advisory Panel. A team drawn from the Bid Team and the Bid Group made this on 8 October 2002.

9   Following guidance from the Government Office of the West Midlands that it could not directly use EU resources in its Capital of Culture bidding campaign (a restriction that did not seem to affect Liverpool's campaign as it used a EU logo on its campaign materials to acknowledge that it received funding from this source). The other partners were Birmingham City Council, Birmingham Arts Marketing (BAM) and West Midlands Arts. The role of the project in supporting the bid is acknowledged in BAM's annual report: 'The small Capitalising on Culture team is working closely with the "be in birmingham 2008" campaign to ensure that the artistic and cultural strengths of the region are fully recognised in the race for ECOC 2008.'

10 The bid had always been designed as a city and regional bid.

11 The exhibition was launched in London on 20 February 2003.

12 www.papicselect.com

Chapter 14

Without Borders

Vanley Burke

After 30 years documenting the West Indian community in Birmingham, I felt the need to include and document other cultures as well. Recently there have been a number of new people who have settled in Birmingham after escaping persecution in their own country – immigrants from the 'Third World' thankful for the opportunity to start their lives again. I have chosen to look at the Somalians and Kurds as well as those who were here in earlier years. These photographs are a way of showing how each respective group have adapted within their city and transformed their environments.

14.1
Mosque under construction, Lozells Road, 2003

14.2
Pakistani men enjoying a game of Kabbadi, Canon Hill Park, 2002

14.3
Upper Sutton Street, Aston, 2001

14.4
Somali Internet café, Stratford Road, 2003

14.5
Somali shopowner, Stratford Road, 2003

14.6
Somali shops, Stratford Road, 2003

14.7
**Somali women,
Birchfield Road,
Lozells, 2002**

14.8
**Afro-Caribbeans,
Handsworth Park,
2002**

14.9
Centenary Square, 2002

14.10 *(left)*
Subway, Birchfield Road, 2003

14.11 *(above)*
**Kurds in St Theresa's,
Handsworth, 2003**

14.12 *(below)*
**First Kurdish supermarket in
Handsworth, Rookery Road,
2003**

14.13
Kurds in St Theresa's, 2003

14.14
St Theresa's, 2003

14.15
The President Saddam Hussein Mosque, Birchfield, 2003

14.16
Soho Road, 2002

14.17
**Gurdwara on Rookery Road,
2002**

14.8
**Public gathering to protest against
violence in Aston, Aston Villa
Football Ground, 2003**

Chapter 15

Into the New, New, Old City

Maria Balshaw

As a child my heart always lifted when I caught sight of Spaghetti Junction – it meant only ten more minutes to my Nan's house and the excitement of a city where things were made and the world was concrete, large and loud. My brother solemnly announced the appearance of 'Fort Dunplop' on the horizon as his first contribution to a repertoire of family jokes about the industrial Midlands that was home to both sides of my extended family. All very unlike the suburban order of the new town my parents had relocated to. This nostalgic love of the networks of roads that make up Birmingham's distinctive concrete modernism stays with me to this day, but I'm aware it's not a widely shared experience even amongst Brummies. As many of the essays in this collection attest, Birmingham is again giving itself a makeover, attempting to get out from under its concrete brutalism. We are seeing those Liam Kennedy calls the commercial imagineers project a sexy new Birmingham; a cosmopolitan centre, tolerant of its many communities with good shopping and spaces for people to walk. Birmingham is experiencing an unprecedented urban renaissance; the city of roads is racing to realize its potential as city of culture – city of learning – city of diversity. A Creative City, to use one of Birmingham City Council's many epithets, where the requirements of twenty-first-century creative life, from lattes to 'authentic' South Asian food, lively gay village, independent music and arts sectors and loft apartments are all making their presence felt on and in the (post) industrial cityscape of Birmingham (Florida 2002).[1]

At the same time we are also seeing a sly revaluing of the recent past that the newly minted creative city might wish to disavow. Imagineers of a rather different stripe are actively reclaiming Birmingham's iconic roads as this city's most distinctive contribution to visual urban culture in the early twenty-first century. We see, within Birmingham's current projection of its

15.1
**Bank Restaurant
advertising,
Birmingham, 2003**

'future', Spaghetti Junction as concrete spaghetti on Bank's lavish menus.[2] In Tom Merilion's hands the giant roads on stilts become a toy town map with models like highly coloured candy. His images filter the dirt and the noise out in a way which gives us the city of roads afresh but also suggests how the planners and architects of Birmingham's concrete futurism wipe it nearly clean of people. At the same time his remaking and revisiting of Birmingham's industrial spaces also mirror my own nostalgic engagement with the Birmingham of the 1970s.[3] His Birmingham is one shown in filigree delicacy from a soaring bird's eye view that gives us the city as a whole but distances us from the engaging disjunctions of Birmingham at street level.

If we look to the work of Birmingham urban landscape painter, Reuben Colley, here too we see Spaghetti Junction and Birmingham's underpasses and expressways; the stylistic echoes of Edward Hopper's work underscoring the Americanism of much of Birmingham's visual identity. Colley's work (see the essay by Deborah Parsons in this volume) moves toward a romantic modernity that serves a useful function for the commercial remakers of Birmingham. It is notable that Colley's images of the regenerated canals, the Mailbox redevelopment and the Rotunda have been extensively used in advertising for the 'new Birmingham'. At the present time (the winter of 2002) disembarking at Euston Station in London, having

15.2
Tom Merilion, Spaghetti Junction, 2000

travelled from Birmingham, one is greeted by a billboard poster for the city of roads featuring one of Colley's Mailbox images, advertising the leisure complex as the latest must-see destination (an oft ironic joke for commuters who rely on the far from reliable Virgin train service between London and Birmingham). (See colour plate 15)

I should say at this point that I use the term 'imagineering' as a productively ambiguous term. It condenses current attempts to remake and rebuild Birmingham as a cultural, economic and regeneration project and stands as the latest move in a long and venerable history of Birmingham as the capital of getting things done. In this sense I see the term having a positive valence. On the other hand, as Liam Kennedy and Joe Holyoak suggest in this volume, it points to the extent that Birmingham's current rebuilding is driven by commercial image-makers whose motives and intentions have little to do with social justice or cultural entitlement. The term imagineers as a useful one, because it expresses the ambivalent processes that are driving urban change in Birmingham currently and might offer us a way of engaging with the city's complex visual cultures.

This collection itself intervenes in discourses of critical–visual revaluation of Birmingham's industrial transport history with the visual essays by Graham Gussin and Nigel Prince and Vanley Burke standing in dialogue with the text and analysis of the collection. The collection becomes part of a process of critical–creative imagineering; an engagement with the uneven and disjunctive process of urban regeneration and visual meaning making. In the words of another of Birmingham's creative meaning makers, theatre and live arts company Stan's Cafe,[4] what we are seeing here is the 'new, new, old city'. This essay will be an engagement with the work of Stan's Cafe, and with some work which has taken place through the Department of Culture, Media and Sport (DCMS) funded Creative Partnerships programme,[5] as one example of how we might try to tell the story of the city from beneath the flyover, engaging with pedestrian perspectives and the view from the car, with Birmingham in old and new versions, with a city that more than most is characterized not just by what Liam Kennedy in his introduction calls 'creative destruction' but with creative disjunction, between times, spaces, identities and communities.

Divercity[6]

It is a fact much noted by city image-makers, artists and citizens alike that Birmingham finds its distinctiveness in its diversity (Plant 2003). It is likely to be the first major majority black and minority ethnic (BME) city in the UK; its school population will be majority BME by the end of this decade; it supports organizations such as SAMPAD, African Cultural Exchange, Chitraleka Dance Company, Jubilee Arts/The Public, the Drum and many others who are noted leaders in culturally diverse cultural production. City of Diversity was the final 'unique selling point' for Birmingham's recent European Capital of Culture bid (see Jane Lutz's essay in this volume). That bid's failure is perhaps related to the difficulty in projecting a singular image of Birmingham that captures this diversity. From the perspective of Birmingham's many local communities (and Birmingham is a city of many highly distinctive neighbourhoods), the difficulty of projecting Birmingham's multiple cultural identities may also be about the lack of engagement (perceived or actual) between the city's high profile, often high cultural city centre-based organizations (from the Hippodrome to the City of Birmingham Symphony Orchestra) and the localities that make up Birmingham's outer inner city. What I want to suggest in this essay is that Birmingham's failure to project a singular image might be its most interesting and provocative feature. As Birmingham fails to impose or project a dominant identity, it offers up a post-industrial, dynamically global and local space through a collage of dominant, emergent and residual historical, geographical and subjective modes.

Birmingham has been a multicultural city of distinctive neighbourhoods for longer than any city except London. It is useful as we attempt to describe and diagnose Birmingham's twenty-first-century visual culture to think back to the 1970s (the formative years for both myself and Tom Merilion). In the 1970s Digbeth belonged to the Irish rather than the burgeoning techno-bohemians who make up the latest wave of incomers to this area. The Chung Ying restaurant was then, as now, the centre of a Chinese section of the city – though in those days without the concrete pagoda and the Arcadian centre. Handsworth was more Afro-Caribbean than it is today, but one still made the trek to the Shalimar restaurant for good Indian food, or drove out of town to the Stratford Road if one wanted to eat the all-in-one-bowl meals we now call baltis. Vanley Burke's photographs in this collection document the latest shifts in community make-up in Handsworth – tracing the recent Somali and Kurdish immigration to Handsworth, Lozells and Aston. Looking back over his thirty-year history of making photos in and around Handsworth reminds us of a continuity of diversity as the experience of this city. It also warns us against seeing black and minority ethnic communities as new, or not connected to Birmingham's past as a manufacturing centre, a place that made things and did things.

What I'm suggesting here is that there is a commonplace interpretation of Birmingham, reinforced (Kennedy 2001) by the common adoption of US urban development models as a framework of understanding for the city, of Birmingham as archetypal post-industrial city. In this understanding Birmingham is cast as a site of manufacture, of heavy industry, where class as a modality of identity predominates. As those industries decline and eventually close, class is replaced by post-industrial modalities of race and ethnicity. This sees Birmingham's experience as of a piece with cities like Detroit and Chicago, where industrial decline leads to white flight from the city centre and the growth of largely non-working non-white communities in the inner city. This may be the experience of some parts of Birmingham (Aston/Lozells, for example), but it is not a useful model if one wishes to tease out continuities over time or to speak about the ways in which Birmingham has remained a city where things are made by many people and communities, even as it has declined as a city of mass manufacture. Over the last few years there has been a lively debate about the need to capture Birmingham's rich community histories, whether one is discussing Birmingham's working-class communities exemplified by Carl Chinn's 'Old Brum' (see Chinn 2000 and 2003) or the experience of Caribbean people coming to Birmingham in the 1950s. Chinn's powerful populist take on local history valorizes working-class solidarity and authenticity and points to the traditions of the (largely white) Birmingham working people as that which is lost or eroded in the rush to celebrate Birmingham as a multicultural city. Leaving aside the extent to which this sidelines the long history of community diversity in Birmingham, this projection of a lost working-class authenticity as the best story Birmingham has to tell has unfortunate echoes of the worst kind of image problems Birmingham faces in national and international terms (see Lutz, this volume).

Birmingham is better modelled as a palimpsest of competing modes, which represent different points of global/local connection, different points of historical time. It is a city that is made very actively by its distinctive communities. These communities grow, make and remake themselves very quickly. Though Balsall Heath and Handsworth may seem to share many similar features in terms of ethnic make-up, they are experienced and project themselves in highly distinctive ways. The predominance of Pakistani families with strong links to Pakistan in Balsall Heath gives us one reason for the high numbers of Internet/phone shops and the preponderance of cheap international phone cards for sale in newsagents. The development of restaurant culture in this part of the city – the so-called 'balti belt' – means it is an area of the city with high visitor numbers (at least on a Friday or Saturday night) and the continued evidence of previous waves of immigrant communities, most particularly through the visual incongruities of halal butchers, Arabic booksellers and sari shops next door to Irish pubs suggests an intercultural dynamic that is characteristically inner city urban (Amin, *et al.* 2000). For recent Pakistani immigrants the experience of living in this locality is likely to be a rather different one, where the local is less significant than pronounced global connections. When pupils at Anderton Park Primary school were asked about the differences between their experience of Balsall Heath and Pakistan, their responses suggested only marginal differences – no traffic lights, better weather – rather than perceptions of fundamental cultural differences.[7] For many of the young people at this school, 99 per cent of whom are of South Asian background,[8] life in Birmingham is experienced through a strongly maintained sense of local Pakistani identity and the cultures and mores of their Pakistani villages and cities are an active constituent of what is means to be a Brummie in this part of town.

Though sharing a relatively similar balance of black and minority ethnic communities, Handsworth presents a rather different scenario. Patterns of Afro-Caribbean then South Asian and now African and East European immigration produce an inter-ethnic, interracial dynamic which has considerable pluses (see, for example, Dave Pollard's discussion of the Sozo collective in this collection) but also produces inter-ethnic tensions which interact with a long and bitter history of racist experiences for many Handsworth communities. Though Handsworth's population is now predominantly South Asian, it maintains a strong sense of itself as an Afro-Caribbean community, supported by venerable culture institutions such as Soho House, a well-developed carnival and artists-in-residence like Vanley Burke and Barbara Walker.

My tracing of these different articulations of the local in Birmingham is to suggest that we need a model of the city that might capture such differences. I am drawn to Raymond William's powerful suggestion that culture as a social system of meaning making should be understood as made up of dominant, emergent and residual cultures, which one might conceive of as competing historical times, held within the present (Williams 1977). Birmingham attempts continually to knock down the old and reinstate a new, better, more polished version of itself. This has been its tendency since at least the nineteenth century. It has been a city which has looked for models, and produced many ideal versions of itself (as Merilion's photos take humour in reminding us) but I would suggest that its greatest success has been in its failure to impose a dominant mode of representation, or even a dominant way of being for the city; for in this failure – in the chinks in the modernist (concrete) visioning – we find the making of competing and disjunctive communities and identities. The city is made in the clash between residual and emergent cultures.

A powerful example of this can be seen in the developing 'learning quarter' of the city in Digbeth. Digbeth has long been the down-at-heel part of town; the city's none too salubrious coach station is there and until recent years it was known mostly for its Irish pubs and their after-hours drinking tolerance. Over the past few years it has become an area which has attracted the urban pioneers; artists, makers, warehouse dwellers who so very frequently act as the vanguards of change in inner city areas (see Shapiro 2000). In predictable fashion this area is now being spruced up – with the Bull Ring redevelopment dramatically changing the way this area connects to the city and a proposed new Richard Rogers library anchoring a (typically Birmingham) new vision of a high tech, multimedia-driven learning quarter. What one does not see in this vision of the area are those elements which make it most dynamic and distinctive; the clash of Birmingham old and new. Digbeth is made up of many warehouses and workshops; the availability of relatively large spaces is one of the attractions of the area for artists and makers. When Stan's Cafe were looking for a new base for the company, the proximity to the noise of car manufacture in their building was a plus rather than a drawback. The Custard Factory arts and media centre, managed workspace such as the Arch or the Bond Gallery complex are all housed in former factory spaces. These spaces fulfil the avant-gardist desire for the edgy urban rendered useful through retrofitting to provide Internet access and gallery space. However, unlike many areas which undergo bohemian makeover Digbeth still makes car parts, church candles, neon signs and cement, bashes metal and does laundry. There is an active rather than uneasy coexistence of old forms of heavy manufacture with new light industries, service sector and the creative sector – both publicly funded and commercial. In Williams' terms we see the coexistence of residual and emergent forms of activity that resist yielding up a dominant mode for the area.

Voodoo City

In the last portion of this essay I want to point to a couple of examples as a way into this creative disjunction. In particular, a series of observations about Stan's Cafe, a theatre company that specializes in sometimes unusual performance installation and live arts work, might offer us some clues about how Birmingham can be understood through a process of creative interventions in meaning making. In Stan's Cafe's engagement with Birmingham as a site of meaning and production we may find a way to engage with Birmingham's multiple historical times and spaces.

Stan's Cafe's company vision statement presents a highly metaphorical vision of their artistic policy and ethos. Pitching themselves as sixteenth-century explorers navigating by the stars, they represent their work as a series of journeys that collect intelligence about navigating the present. Much of this navigation concerns itself with articulating the conditions of urban life in Birmingham, even as the pieces of work rarely appear to be about Birmingham in any obvious or manifest way. So, their performance piece, *Voodoo City* (1995) starts from the image of a woman who threw herself and her baby to her death off the top of a tower block (a story taken from a newspaper – not a Birmingham story, though the imagery of the opening 'spell' in the piece originates on the streets of Balsall Heath in Birmingham).[9] Another piece, *Ocean of Storms* (1996) juxtaposes the voices of two quasi-angels who are searching for a small child lost in the city, with the dialogue between ground control and a space shuttle during a potentially fatal re-entry to Earth.[10] Much of the dialogue for this piece was generated by James Yarker, artistic director of Stan's Cafe, as he rode the circular 11c bus around Birmingham. In the early days of the company the relationship with Birmingham was still more materially grounded. As a small, experimental company without revenue funding through public bodies such as the Arts Council, sets and props, as well as spaces for performance, were often made out of the discarded leftovers of Birmingham. In Yarker's words, when furniture was put out on the street to die, it often experienced its final death as part of a Stan's performance.[11]

There is a process of making here that seems characteristically Birmingham. Yarker puts it thus: 'I came to Birmingham from the South where nothing was made, to a city where real things were made every day and I have always been fascinated with this.'[12] In engaging at a practical and metaphorical level with processes of making, Stan's Cafe's work engages with old and new versions of Birmingham. Yarker comments: 'The heart of Stan's Cafe lies in Balsall Heath. The clash of cultures, impoverished means and surreal spectacle of this area can be found traced across the company's work.'[13] In the terms sketched out above, their work presents a dialogue between residual and emergent articulations of Birmingham. This is well caught in one of their more light-hearted pieces, *Space Station* (2002), where the company were commissioned (as part of Jubilee Arts/The Public's Platforms project) to install their own (space) station platform, 'EarthNorthStation', on the Black Country metro line, just past Wednesbury, manned by astronauts who tried and ultimately succeeded through the course of the day to board the train.[14] Though whimsical, the performance engaged with many levels of authority and many processes of meaning-making in the city. Negotiations with the Department of Transport were needed in order to install the platform and stop the train at an unauthorized point to allow the astronauts to board at the end of the day. Train conductors had to become semi-official gallery guides as passengers encountered the performance (and the others that were spread out along the metro line between West Bromwich and Wednesbury). The piece also asked casual passers-by to make a judgement about their own navigation around the city. The absurd proposition of astronauts carrying briefcases failing to catch the train wraps up everyday frustrations of commuters with hope and cynicism about new 'space age' technologies like Global Positioning Systems (GPS), which will apparently deliver us from the urban horrors of rush hour gridlock. This is an issue all too real for Birmingham citizens as the city of roads perpetually threatens to turn into the city of traffic jams.

Walking with Your Eyes Closed

Stan's Cafe's process of making performance through and in Birmingham offers a way of seeing and engaging with a multiply constituted city. To close, I would like to offer some reflections on a piece of work produced by Stan's Cafe as part of the Creative Partnerships Birmingham programme. Stan's Cafe were tasked to develop a day-long experience that would explore the role of risk-taking in creative learning for teachers from the 26 schools working as part of this initiative. They were also asked to make this

15.3
Stan's Cafe, *Space Station*, 2002

exploration a chance for teachers to explore Birmingham city centre as a site of creative engagement. Their response was a Risk Day, where teachers working in pairs were given a series of choices that guided their navigation around and through Birmingham city centre, collecting observations and encounters, to an end point in Digbeth at the Chuck Works (Stan's Cafe's base) and then the Custard Factory, where the Creative Partnerships office is located. It was a walking tour without a definite map, where the journey to the end point could vary dramatically depending on the choices and responses of the participants. Stan's Cafe had devised a series of encounters with aspects of Birmingham, some familiar and some arcane. So participants were directed to the Waterstones bookshop that overlooks the new Bull Ring area and told to read a middle section of a novel by Birmingham novelist Jim Crace that describes the Bull Ring market. Another instruction was to listen to a track from the Streets album that describes life in the high rise blocks in Small Heath. Still another asked participants to put on a blindfold and feel their way across the bridge over the A38. It is this image that ties together much of what I am trying to suggest in this piece. Blindfold, the teachers had to feel their way across the bridge accompanied by the sound of that most familiar of Birmingham elements, the rush and roar of the traffic.

15.4
Risk Day in Birmingham, 2003

As the teachers made their way through the city and through their encounters with some of its symbolic representations, from books to buildings like the Rotunda, they were invited to reflect on the discontinuous elements of a city 'made' by people. Without becoming *flâneurs* – Birmingham it seems to me is always going to be a city which resists *flânerie*, however much it changes its built environment to welcome the walker – the teachers saw the city from a different perspective by being active walkers. Their engagement with their surroundings asked them to encounter many articulations of what Birmingham means in 2003 and their connection with the human complexity of the city stands in opposition to the heightened modernist sensibility of the *flâneur* (but for more on this, see Parsons in this volume). The diversity of the experiences (from climbing on to the roof of the Chuck Works to discover a bottle of champagne and a Polaroid camera, to ordering food in Chinese in Chinatown, to hearing poetry while sitting on a city bench) resists the tendency to romanticize the city as a space of ruin or nostalgia or futurist regeneration and focuses on Birmingham as a site of disjunctive discourses of urbanity. At the end of the Risk Day, Stan's Cafe presented a performance text created by Craig Stephens and based on the observations collected by the teacher navigators. This essay will close with this poem, as a slightly silly but also profound engagement with Birmingham's visual cultures. It offers a vision for the future of the city that is not caught up with creative destruction, not dreamed up by commercial imagineers, but in tune with the ongoing work of creative imagineers who, in the words of Stan's Cafe's performance, 'make it, who make it into the city everyday, who make it into Birmingham everyday'.[15] From this (blindfold) perspective, it is precisely Birmingham's failure to articulate a dominant view of itself that gives it an edge as a city of makers, of things, histories, communities and ideas, with all the conflict between residual and emergent elements that this must entail. Birmingham will continue to remake itself, but it will be the incomplete nature of this transformation that means its future will always be in the making.

THE ZONE OF THE UNKNOWN

A–Z, 1 to 15. Into the zone. Joining up the pages
Past the station, down the ramp, under the Rotunda, opposite HMV, the sound of music . . .
Is it the sound of the streets? Can't make him out, he's wearing a top with the hood up, making the sounds, saying the sounds of the city.
A to Z, 1 to 15. Into the unknown
Standing near the axis of it all, feet scraping, traffic humming, the song of the fanbelt
Seeing the sides of buildings not seen before, the
invisible city . . . but for the people

But for the people who make it, who make it into the city everyday, who make it into Birmingham everyday.

The couple on their way to the hills, clandestine, hand in hand, the city below, only they know.

The overweight, overheated lorry driver. Too many breakfasts in Mr Egg.

The lads leaving it behind, for hills and lakes and boats.

The toothbrush salesman on his way to Redditch, wishing it was him, not Jim, at the ICC for the dental hygienists' convention

A to Z, 1 to 15. Into the new, new old city.

Where the corrugated canal ripples past cement work chimney stack,

Merlin and Fastblast, Latif and Rose, names to conjure, beds to guitars, cars to conservatories.

Where the jet train roars and cars lie crushed and the streets are paved with . . .

But there's beauty . . . in the walls that grow trees and sprout verse.

In the crisp packets waltzing in the wind

In the barbed wire sculpture on Banbury Street.

A to Z, 1 to 15. Linking the lines

Into the dark, don't turn back,

There are no dead ends. Head for the light, follow the stars,

Look for the sparks . . .

Notes

1   Richard Florida is currently the most prominent of writers extolling the economic power of the creative class within a knowledge-driven urban economy, but the work of Charles Landry and associates at Comedia (see Landry 1995 and 2000) has probably had more direct influence on Birmingham's politicians and planners. The city's Economic Development Unit recently launched its own Creative City strategy (Birmingham City Council 2003), which outlines economic support for creative quarters in the city, sadly without really addressing the human dimensions of the creative city.

2   A large fork hovers over the extreme aerial view of Spaghetti Junction as if to suggest how easily we might consume the city as image.

3   See the poem written by Merilion as an introduction to the exhibition catalogue for *The People and the City: A Cultural Portrait of Birmingham*, Brian Griffin and Tom Merilion (Griffin and Merilion 2003). It is probably no mere coincidence that Tom and I are the same age.

4   Stan's Cafe at www.stanscafe.co.uk. The company have been in existence since 1991 and are currently based at The Chuck Works in Digbeth in Birmingham.

5   Creative Partnerships is a national programme funded by DCMS through Arts Council England and the Department for Education and Skills to bring the creative and cultural sector into partnership with the education sector in order to expand the range of creative learning opportunities offered to young people in areas of social, economic and cultural disadvantage. See www.creative-partnerships.com.

6   The misspelling gives us the title of the city's marketing drive to support more commercial professionals from black and minority ethnic communities.

7   The example comes from a storytelling and dance project led by Birmingham Royal Ballet with six Creative Partnerships schools from the Balsall Heath/Kings Heath area.

8   The official school figures are 89 per cent Pakistani, 7 per cent Bangledeshi, 3 per cent Indian, 1 per cent Other.

9 See www.stanscafe.co.uk/voodoo.html.

10 See www.stanscafe.co.uk/ocean.html.

11 See www.stanscafe.co.uk/qwhere.html.

12 James Yarker, personal interview with author, 2003.

13 See www.stanscafe.co.uk/vooscript.html for more on this.

14 See www.stanscafe.co.uk/spacestation.html.

15 It also is a vision of the city which, against the currently fashionable drive toward a know-ledge-driven creative city, posits a city organized in spatial and temporal terms around the social interactions and discontinuities of its multiple citizenry (see Amin, Massey *et al.* 2000).

Bibliography

Advantage West Midlands (2001) *Agenda for Action*, Birmingham: Advantage West Midlands.

Amin, A., Massey, D. and Thrift, N. (2000) *Cities for the Many Not the Few*, Bristol: The Policy Press.

Anon (1839) 'Daguerreotype in Birmingham', *The Birmingham Gazette*, 26 October.

Balshaw, M. and Kennedy, L. (eds) (2000) *Urban Space and Representation*, London: Pluto Press.

Barber, A. (2001) *The ICC, Birmingham: a catalyst for urban renaissance*, Birmingham Centre for Urban and Regional Studies, University of Birmingham.

BBC 2 (1991) *From Cars to Conventions, Birmingham*, BBC Television.

Benjamin, W. (1973) *Charles Baudelaire: a lyric poet in the era of high capitalism*, trans. Harry Zohn, London: Verso.

Bianchini, F. and Parkinson, M. (eds) (1993) *Cultural Policy and Urban Regeneration: the western European experience*, Manchester: Manchester University Press.

Birmingham Arts Marketing (2002) *Birmingham Arts Marketing Annual Review 2002*, Birmingham: Birmingham Arts Marketing.

Birmingham City Council (1993) *The Birmingham Plan*, Birmingham: Birmingham City Council.

Birmingham City Council (2001a) *Distinctively Birmingham: a local cultural strategy for the city*, Birmingham: Birmingham City Council.

Birmingham City Council (2001b) *Highbury 3: dynamic, diverse, different*, Birmingham: Birmingham City Council.

Birmingham City Council (2002) *Community Strategy*, Birmingham: Birmingham City Council.

Birmingham City Council (2003) *The Creative City*, Birmingham: Birmingham City Council.

Birmingham for the People (1989) *The People's Plan for the Bull Ring*, Birmingham: Birmingham for the People.

Birmingham Post (1991) 'Royal visitors set the seal on city's rebirth', 12 June.

Birmingham Post (2002) 'Capital of culture: hard work begins now', 31 October.

Bloomfield, J. and Bianchini F. (2002) *Planning for the Cosmopolitan City: a research report for Birmingham City Council*, Comedia in association with the International Cultural Planning and Policy unit, DeMontfort University, Stroud: Comedia.

Bournville Village Trust (1941) *When We Build Again: a study based on research into conditions of living and working in Birmingham*, London: George Allen & Unwin.

Boyle, M. and Hughes, G. (1991) 'The politics of the representations of the "real": discourses from the left on Glasgow's role as City of Culture', *Area*, 23: 217–28.

Briggs, A. (1956) *Friends of the People: the centenary history of Lewis's*, London: B. T. Batsford.

Brown, R. E. and Redmayne, P. (1943) *Changing Britain: illustrating the Industrial Revolution 1750–1940*, Birmingham: Cadbury Brothers.

Cadbury, P. S. (1952) *Birmingham – Fifty Years On*, Birmingham: Bournville Village Trust.

Caffyn, A. and Lutz, J. (1999) 'Developing the heritage tourism product in multi-ethnic cities', *Tourism Management* 20: 215–21.

Caiger-Smith, M. (1992) *Site Work: architecture in photography since early modernism*, London: Photographer's Gallery.

Calvino, I. (1974) *Invisible Cities*, London: Secker and Warburg.

Chambers, I. (1991) *Border Dialogues: journeys in postmodernity*, London: Routledge.

Chatwin, J. (1997) 'Viewpoint: Brindleyplace implementation', *Urban Design Quarterly* 62: 12–14.

Chinn, C. (1991) *Homes for People: 100 years of council housing in Birmingham*, Birmingham, Birmingham City Council.

Chinn, C. (2000) *Brum and Brummies*, Studley: Brewin Books.

Chinn, C. (2003) *Birmingham Irish: making our mark*, Birmingham: Birmingham City Council.

Clohessy, L. (1994) '''Dublin 1991' – European City of Culture', in U. Kockel (ed.) *Culture, Tourism and Development: the case for Ireland*, Liverpool: Liverpool University Press.

Cowan, M. (2000) 'The New Brum', *The Evening Mail*, 18 July.

Crossick, G. and Jaumain, S. (1999) *Cathedrals of Consumption: the European department store, 1850–1939*, Aldershot: Ashgate.

DCMS (2000) *European Capital of Culture 2008: criteria and information for applicants*, London: Department for Culture, Media and Sports.

DCMS (2001) *Creating Opportunities: guidance for local authorities in England on local cultural strategies*, London: Department for Culture, Media and Sports.

Ellis, J. (2001) 'Sozo Collective: Intervention', *MADE Newsletter*, 2: 10.

Evans, G. (2001) *Cultural Planning*, London: Routledge.

Evening Mail (1991) 'Jewel in our crown', 28 March.

Eyles, J. and Peace, W. (1990) 'Signs and symbols in Hamilton: an iconology of Steeltown', *Geografiska Annaler*, 72: 73–88.

Florida, R. (2002) *The Rise of the Creative Class*, New York: Basic Books.

French, P. (1999) 'Felicia's Journey', the *Observer*, 17 March.

Fussell, P. (1980) *Abroad: British literary travelling between the wars*, Oxford: Oxford University Press.

Gehl, J. (1996) *Life Between Buildings*, 3rd edn, Copenhagen: Arkitektens Forlag.

Gilloch, G. (2002) *Walter Benjamin: critical constellations*, Oxford: Polity Press.

Glancey, J. (2002) 'Rainbow warrior', The *Guardian*, 18 February.

Gold, J. and Ward, S. (eds) (1994) *Place Promotion: the use of publicity and marketing to sell towns and regions*, Chichester: John Wiley.

Goodey, B. (1994) 'Art-ful places: public art to sell public spaces?', in J. Gold and S. Ward (eds) *Place Promotion: the use of publicity and marketing to sell towns and regions*, Chichester: John Wiley.

Goodey, B., Duffett, A. W., Gold, J. R. and Spencer, D. (1971) *City Scene: an exploration of the image of central Birmingham as seen by area residents*, Birmingham: Centre for Urban and Regional Studies, University of Birmingham.

Griffin, B. and Merilion, T. (2003) *The People and the City*, Birmingham: Seeing the Light.

Grimley, T. (2002) 'What makes the city so memorable, asks selection panel chief', *The Birmingham Post*, 31 October.

Grosse, K. (2002) *Cool Puppen*, Munich: Minerva.

Hall, C.M. (1992) *Hallmark Tourist Events: impacts, management, and planning*, London: Belhaven.

Hall, T. (1995) 'Public art, urban image', *Town and Country Planning*, 64, 4: 122–3.

Hall, T. (2001) *Urban Geography*, London: Routledge.

Hall, T. and Robertson, I. (2001) 'Public art and urban regeneration: advocacy, claims and critical debates', *Landscape Research*, 26,1: 5–26.

Hallett, M. (1986) 'Imagining the city', *British Journal of Photography*, 28 November: 1369–70.

Hartnell, R. (1995) 'Art and civic culture in Birmingham in the late nineteenth century', *Urban History* 22, 2: 230–42.

Hastilow, N (1991) 'Proud day for nation's most progressive city', *Birmingham Post*, 12 June.

Hedges, N. (1991) *From the Centre: living through change in an industrial society 1965–1990*, Wolverhampton: Light House.

Heikkinen, T. (2000) 'In from the margins: the City of Culture 2000 and the image transformation of Helsinki', *International Journal of Cultural Policy*, 6: 201–18.

Higgott, A. (2000) 'Birmingham: building the modern city', in T. Deckker (ed.) *The Modern City Revisited*, London: Spon.

Highmore, B. (2002) *Everyday Life and Cultural Theory*, London: Routledge.

Hitters, E. (2000) 'The social and political construction of a European Capital of Culture: Rotterdam 2001', *International Journal of Cultural Policy*, 6: 183–99.

Holyoak, J. (1990) 'Spending on a grand scale', *The Architect's Journal*, 21 November, 9.

Holyoak, J. (2002) 'The redevelopment of Birmingham's Bull Ring: the politics of organized popular involvement in planning', *Scroope* 14: 36–43.

Hopia, N. (2001) 'An analysis of the evaluation of the Scandinavian Cities of Culture: what can UK cities bidding to become European Capital of Culture learn about evaluation from Copenhagen, Stockholm, Helsinki and Bergen?', unpublished MSc dissertation, Centre for Urban and Regional Studies, The University of Birmingham.

Hubbard, P. (1995) 'Re-imaging the city – the transformation of Birmingham's urban landscape', *Geography*, 81: 189–202.

Hubbard, P. (1996) 'Re-imagining the city: the transformation of Birmingham's urban landscape', *Cities*, 12: 243–51.

Hughes, G. (1999) 'Urban revitalization: the use of festive time strategies', *Leisure Studies*, 18: 119–35.

Hughes, H. (2000) *Arts, Entertainment and Tourism*, Oxford: Butterworth-Heinemann.

Ikon (2000) *As It Is*, Birmingham: Ikon Gallery.

Ikon (2001) *Birmingham*, Birmingham: Ikon Gallery.

Jacobs, J. (1961) *The Death and Life of Great American Cities*, New York: Random House.

James, P. (1996) 'Rebuilding the Home Front: photographs by Bill Brandt 1939–1943', *The PhotoHistorian*, London: Historical Group of the Royal Photographic Society.

James, P. (1998) *Coming to Light: Birmingham's photography collections*, Birmingham: Birmingham Libraries.

James, P. (2001) 'Regenerating Birmingham', *DPICT*, 5: 13.

Jeffrey, I. (2001) 'Far and Wide: the city pictures of John Davies', *Portfolio*, 33: 15–17.

Jeffries, S. (2000) 'Spin City', The *Guardian*, 3 January: 16–17.

Judd, D. R. and Fainstein, S. S. (1999) *The Tourist City*, London: Yale University Press.

Kearns, G. and Philo, C. (eds) (1993) *Selling Places: the city as cultural capital, past and present*, Oxford: Pergamon Press.

Kemp, P. (2000) 'Nasty Neighbours', *Sight and Sound*, November: 58–9.

Kennedy, L. (2001) 'How American Is It? Transnational urbanism and the cultural politics of place making,' http://artsweb.bham.ac.uk.49thparallel

Koolhaas, R. (2001) *The Harvard Design School Guide to Modern Shopping*, Köln: Taschen.

Kotler, P., Asplund, C., Rein, I. and Halder, D. (1999) *Marketing Places: Europe*, Harlow: Prentice Hall.

Landry, C. (1995) *The Art of Regeneration: urban renewal through cultural activity*, London: Demos.

Landry, C. (2000) *The Creative City: a toolkit for urban innovators*, London: Earthscan.

Le Corbusier (1967) *The Radiant City: elements of a doctrine of urbanism to be used as the basis for our machine-age civililization*, London: Faber and Faber.

Lefebvre, H. (1991) *The Production of Space*, trans. Donald Nicholson-Smith, Oxford: Blackwell.

Lim, H. (1993) 'Cultural strategies for revitalizing the city: a review and evaluation', *Regional Studies*, 26: 589–95.

Loftman, P. and Nevin, B. (1994) 'Prestige project developments: economic renaissance or economic myth? A case study of Birmingham', *Local Economy*, 8: 307–25.

Loftman, P. and Nevin, B. (1998) 'Pro-growth local economic development strategies: civic promotion and local needs in Britain's second city 1981–1996', in T. Hall and P. Hubbard (eds) *The Entrepreneurial City: geographies of politics, regime and representation*, Chichester: John Wiley.

Lovell, V. (1988) 'Report by the Public Arts Commissions Agency to the Arts Working Party', unpublished.

Lutz, J. (2003) 'Culture and place-marketing: a case study of Birmingham and its bid to become European Capital of Culture in 2008', *The Birmingham Papers*, Birmingham: Birmingham City Council International and European Unit.

Lutz, J., Barber, A., Calcutt, P., Clarke, D. and Turpie, J. (2002) 'The Media Portrayal of the West Midlands', unpublished paper, The Centre for Urban and Regional Studies The University of Birmingham.

Lutz, J. and Ryan, C. (1997) 'Impacts of inner city tourism projects: the case of the international convention centre, Birmingham, UK', in P. Murphy (ed.) *Quality Management in Urban Tourism*, Chichester: John Wiley.

Marriott, O. (1967) *The Property Boom*, London: Hamish Hamilton.

Matarasso, F. (1997) *Use or Ornament: the social impact of participation in the arts*, Stroud: Comedia.

Miles, M. (1997) *Art, Space and the City*, London: Routledge.

Miles, M. (2000) 'A game of appearance: public art and urban development – complicity or sustainability?', in T. Hall and P. Hubbard (eds) *The Entrepreneurial City: geographies of politics, regime, and representation*, Chichester: Wiley.

Morley, C. (1991) 'A symphony of new life for the city', *Birmingham Post*, 13 June.

Myerscough, J. (1992) 'Measuring the impact of the arts: the Glasgow 1990 experience', *Journal of the Market Research Society*, 34: 323–35.

Myerscough, J. (1994) *European Cities of Culture and Cultural Months*, The Network of Cultural Cities of Europe.

Plant, S. (2003) 'The great toyshop of Europe', *New Statesman*, 2 June: 30.

Price, F. (1959) *The New Birmingham*, Birmingham Mail and Public Works Committee, Birmingham City Council.

Redmayne, P. (ed.) (1943) *Our Birmingham: the Birmingham of our forefathers and the Birmingham of our grandsons*, Birmingham: Cadbury Brothers.

Richards, G. (1996) *Cultural Tourism in Europe*, Wallingford: CABI.

Richards, G. (2000) 'The European Capital of Culture Event: strategic weapon in the cultural arms race?', *International Journal of Cultural Policy*, 6: 159–81.

Robins, K. (1994) 'Prisoners of the city: whatever could a postmodern city be?', in E. Carter, J. Donald and J. Squires (eds) *Space and Place: theories of identity and location*, London: Lawrence and Wishart.

Rogers, R. and Power, A. (2000) *Cities for a Small Country*, London: Faber and Faber.

Romney, J. (1999) 'Felicia's Journey', *Sight and Sound*, February: 61.

Roth, S. and Frank, S. (2000) 'Festivalization and the media: Weimar, Cultural Capital of Europe 1999', *International Journal of Cultural Policy*, 6: 219–41.

Sackett, W. J. (1866) *The Buildings of Birmingham Past and Present, Sketched and Described*, Birmingham: Walter J. Sackett.

Sandercock, L. (2002) *Planning for the City of Difference: proceedings of a week of activities Monday 21–Friday January 2002*, Birmingham: Birmingham City Council.

Sargent, A. (1996) 'More than just the sum of its parts: cultural policy and planning in Birmingham', *International Journal of Cultural Policy*, 2, 2: 303–25.

Shapiro, S. (2000) '"Whose Fucking Park? Our Fucking Park!": Bohemian Brummaires (Paris 1848/East Village 1988), gentrification, and the representation of AIDS', in M. Balshaw and L. Kennedy (eds) *Urban Space and Representation*, London: Pluto Press.

Shaylor, G. (1989) 'Public art and urban design: funding and advocacy in the United Kingdom', in British and American Arts Association (eds) *Arts and the Changing City: an agenda for urban regeneration*, London: British and American Arts Association.

Shields, R. (ed.) (1992) *Lifestyle Shopping: the subject of consumption*, London: Routledge.

Short, J. R. (1998) *The Urban Order*, Oxford: Blackwell.

Short, J. R., Benton, L. M., Luce, W. N. and Walton, J. (1993) 'Reconstructing the image of an industrial city', *Annals of the Association of American Geographers*, 83: 207–24.

Sjoholt, P. (1999) 'Culture as a strategic development device: the role of "European Cities of Culture", with particular reference to Bergen', *European Urban and Regional Studies*, 6: 339–47.

Sorkin, M. (1992) *Variations on a Theme Park: the new American city and the end of public space*, New York: Hill and Wang.

Sutcliffe, A. (1970) *A History of Birmingham*, Oxford: Oxford University Press.

Upton, C. (1993) *A History of Birmingham*, Chichester: Phillimore.

Ward, S. V. (1998) *Selling Places: the marketing and promotion of towns and cities 1850–2000*, London: E&FN Spon.

Webster, F. (2001) 'Re-inventing place: Birmingham as an informational city?', *City*, 5: 27–46

Weideger, P. (1991) 'Larger than life tribute to Brum's golden age', The *Independent*, 8 June.

West Midland Group (1948) *Conurbation: a planning survey of Birmingham and the Black Country*, London: The Architectural Press.

West Midlands Life (2001) *West Midlands Regional Cultural Strategy*, Birmingham: West Midlands Life.

Wiener, M. (1981) *English Culture and Decline of the Industrial Spirit 1850–1980*, Harmondsworth: Penguin

Williams, R. (1958) *Culture and Society 1780–1950*, London: Chatto and Windus.

Williams, R. (1976) *Keywords*, Glasgow: Collins.

Williams, R. (1977) *Marxism and Literature*, Oxford: Oxford University Press.

Wishart, R. (1991) 'Fashioning the Future: Glasgow', in M. Fisher and U. Owen (eds) *Whose Cities?*, London: Penguin.

Zukin, S. (1988) *Loft Living: culture and capital in urban change*, London: Radius.

Zukin, S. (1995) *The Cultures of Cities*, Oxford: Blackwell.

Zukin, S. (1996) 'Space and symbols in an age of decline', in A. King (ed.) *Re-Presenting the City: ethnicity, capital and culture in the twenty-first century metropolis*, Basingstoke: Macmillan.

Index